# Wonderfully Made

*The Testimony of a Forgiven Woman*

NEVA ANN CAIRCO

Photography by Elaine Douglas



WestBow Press books may be ordered through booksellers or by contacting:

WestBow Press
A Division of Thomas Nelson & Zondervan
1663 Liberty Drive
Bloomington, IN 47403
www.westbowpress.com
1 (866) 928-1240



ISBN: 978-1-9736-5215-1 (sc)
ISBN: 978-1-9736-5214-4 (hc)
ISBN: 978-1-9736-5216-8 (e)

Library of Congress Control Number: 2019901092

Print information available on the last page.

WestBow Press rev. date: 2/23/2019

***Wonderfully Made*** is *a rare thing—a book that addresses a hot-button issue from a faith-based perspective, but manages to do so without a hint of preachiness or off-putting self-righteousness. Author Neva Ann Cairco skillfully weaves the heartbreaking tale of her tragic personal choices and the ultimate triumph of God's forgiving grace. Abortion is a topic not often publicly discussed outside the political arena.* ***Wonderfully Made*** *brings the discussion inward, to a personal place of pain, brokenness, and healing. This book will resonate with anyone who has ever been affected by the abortion experience, whether personally or peripherally. Its message of tenderness and healing is a much-needed balm from the heart of God for a deep wound that too often goes unacknowledged.*
—Amy Thomas

*This is such a beautiful story of God's healing, forgiveness and restoration. Neva's transparency will be a blessing to those who need to hear a story of God's great love. Finding our value and worth in Christ is our only hope.* ***Wonderfully Made*** *clearly makes that truth the most important principle of life. I agree "God does not waste anything."*
—Bishop Mark Leonhardt, Pastor,
Fort Mill Church of God

# Contents

# *Preface*

This book was not my idea! Now, don't get me wrong, I'm willing to follow the Holy Spirit where He leads me. I'm open to doing whatever He wants me to do. But never in my wildest dreams did I think that I would ever write a book like this.

Let me explain. I have been a Christian since 1988. Admittedly, from time to time I have toyed with the idea of writing a book. But over the past couple of years, this desire seemed to grow. I began to experience recurring thoughts about writing. There were even times when people would make statements about how I should write a book, maybe an autobiography, but I would remind myself that my life really isn't that interesting. So maybe, I thought, I should write a devotional book with inspirational writings and encouraging biblical references. But there didn't seem to be time in my busy schedule to create such a composition. I *never* entertained the thought of writing a book about my deepest, secret sin, or a book that would expose old wounds and dig up old memories, or a book that would reveal a sin that is only spoken of in hushed whispers.

You see, I learned early on in my Christian walk that there seemed to be what I called taboo sins. You know, those sins that only you and God know and talk about. You don't discuss *those* sins with anyone because to share them would expose you. Then you would have to deal with the possibility that others might not relate. They might not understand. They might even condemn you.

Quite frankly, I wasn't willing to risk all that. Yes, I know that the Bible tells us, "Therefore, there is now no condemnation for those who are in Christ Jesus" (Romans 8:1 NIV), but I wasn't willing to chance it on someone who may not have embraced this truth. The embarrassment and pain would be more than I could bear. So like I said, writing a book about my secret sin and exposing my journey so vulnerably was not my idea.

So why write it now? Well, after attending a women's conference in 2017, it became infinitely clear that those thoughts about writing were a prompting of the Holy Spirit. He wasn't toying with me at all. The truth was that He was doing a new thing! In Isaiah 43:18–19, the prophet Isaiah tells the nation of Israel that God is going to restore her after her time of rebellion. "Forget the former things; do not dwell on the past. See, I am doing a new thing! Now it springs up; do you not perceive it? I am making a way in the wilderness and streams in the wasteland" (NIV).

God's intention wasn't that I write this book to just dredge up my past. He was going to use my "wilderness and wasteland" experience to communicate to His children the new thing He has for them. He has everything. He wants everything! The old and new; good and bad; easy and hard; happy and sad—He wants everything. He wastes nothing! He wants to remove everything from those dark places in our hearts and minds. He wants to place them in the light for healing and restoration.

So here I am, writing the book that He wants me to write, in the manner He wants it written, to the children He has selected. This book is being written as the result of a commission given to me at that retreat on Saturday, October 22, 2017.

And finally, I find myself wanting to know why He chose me. Like I said earlier, my life really isn't that interesting. My Christian walk would seem ordinary to most. So why would He choose me? I'm reminded of the verse found in 1 Corinthians, where Paul was telling the believers in the Corinthian church that God uses the simple. He reminds them that it wasn't the scholar or philosopher that God used to reveal Himself. It was those people who didn't require miracles or profound wisdom. It was the weak and lowly people that God used to demonstrate His wisdom, power, and might. First Corinthians 1:27 says, "But God chose the foolish things of the world to shame the wise; God chose the weak things of the world to shame the strong" (NIV). Therefore no one can boast about their own righteousness or holiness. He is sovereign in all things.

He has made it clear to me that He wants to share what He has done in my life. He wants to reveal how He uses our brokenness to create profound breakthroughs in each of our lives. When the broken are healed, God's glory is most wonderfully demonstrated and celebrated.

To His honor and glory, amen.

# Introduction

The topic of this book is not a comfortable one. Clearly, this book is not intended to be light reading. When it comes to addressing my personal sins, I have frequently found myself shying away from sharing them. I would find it too painful, too difficult to openly confront them.

But that is exactly what our loving heavenly Father wants for us. He wants us to see how mighty He is. He wants us to receive His life-changing healing. He wants us to be free from all bondage. He wants to remove the guilt and shame associated with sin's rebellion and self-reliance. And that can come only when we are willing to open ourselves up, realize the truth from His perspective, accept His forgiveness, and allow Him to begin the healing process in our lives.

As I look back on my life's journey, I have spent many hours running away from the truth, covering up, and convincing myself that my sinful actions were justified. In so doing, I blinded myself to the true nature of my sin. I became trapped in a web of deceit. I found myself living a life under the pretense that all was well when, in reality, I was privately dying inside from the decay left behind in the wake of my sin.

In an effort to wade through the pain, I tried to convince myself that my transgressions really were not that bad. I would attempt to minimize their impact on me by trying to prioritize the gravity of my sins. Some seemed to be minor in nature, whereas others seemed more serious. It occurred to me that those sins listed in the Ten Commandments carried a higher level of shame. Idolatry, adultery, theft, and murder are top contenders. Even so, I was clever to quickly rationalize my actions. I would even find ways to explain why I was justified in making choices that lead to sinful activities. My love of money and success appeared normal. Wasn't that the whole point of life—to live successful, productive lives? Then there was the argument that everyone around me was striving for a better life, eliminating any and all obstacles that may come along the way. When it came to my interactions with others, it felt natural to engage in relationships on my terms. I knew what was best for me, and I had a responsibility to make sure those desires were met. As long as other people were filling my needs, all would be fine; if not, well, I would either need to find a solution or move on. Then there was the desire to have whatever I wanted, regardless of the consequences. Surely the benefits of obtaining my desires would outweigh any consequences that might arise. I believed I was able to control my life and whatever it brought me.

But there it was—the very core sin growing inside of me that I didn't recognize. Little did I know at the time that it would ultimately end in death. That hidden sin began to override my life in ways unimaginable. The desire to control my life and my surroundings became my lifestyle. The Bible tells us, "There is a way which seems right to a man, but its end is the way to death" (Proverbs 14:12 ESV). Clearly, I believed my way was right. I had become an expert at relying on my own strategies. Although that approach to life worked for a while, there came a time when the truth of my choices—the reality of my actions—became clear to me. I came to myself, if you will. My way did lead to death! Not just my spiritual death but, tragically, the death of my firstborn.

That was the one sin that I could never seem to justify. No matter how hard I tried, no matter how clever I thought I was, the pain of that choice would not go away. The shame and guilt were so great that I couldn't make it right. The core of that decision came out of the foundational theme of my life. It was the original sin we see in the Garden of Eden. It was the sin of not trusting God and the rebellion of self-reliance.

"Don't worry, God. I've got this."

I understand that the topic of abortion can be seen as controversial. It encompasses social, political, and spiritual matters. In my life experience, I have found it to be a far more dire matter. I say this because it speaks directly to the condition of our hearts, not the condition of our social class or politics. This reaches into eternity. That is why it is so important that we take time to really consider the truth concerning this choice from God's point of view.

For some people, the choice is too tough to grasp. It is a choice far beyond any level of reason. But for those of us who have had an abortion or know someone who has, we are intimately aware of what it is. We know what it is to be tormented as we privately wrestle with our confusion regarding the part we played. Many may find it impossible to discuss, so we hide it; it becomes our wretched secret. The fact that we are not able to discuss it makes matters worse. Our silence keeps it in the dark and robs us of our healing. The more we try to cover up our sin, the more we will continue to live in the bondage of that sin.

The good news, however, is that God has a better way of handling our brokenness. He wants to shed light on our hidden things so we can live free and fruitful lives. "But everything exposed by the light becomes visible—and everything that is illuminated becomes a light. This is why it is said: Wake up, sleeper, rise from the dead, and Christ will shine on you" (Ephesians 5:13–14 NIV).

The Word teaches in James that the more we share and bring those hidden things out of the darkness and into the light of God's love, the more we will share in His healing. James 5:15–16 states, "And the prayer offered in faith will make the sick person well; the Lord will raise them up. If they have sinned, they will be forgiven. Therefore confess your sins to each other and pray for each other so that you may be healed. The prayer of a righteous person is powerful and effective" (NIV).

We need to begin our healing by trusting God and His great love and mercy. I don't ever remember hearing a testimony from anyone about how God released them from the emotional and spiritual consequences of their abortion experience. The Word teaches us that our victory over sin's curse is found in our willingness to open ourselves to God's grace and mercy and share the good news of our healing. Revelation 12:11 says, "They triumphed over him by the blood of the Lamb and by the word of their testimony; they did not love their lives so much as to shrink from death" (NIV).

This book is about sharing my testimony so that you will experience your victory through the powerful, life-changing forgiveness, grace, and abounding love found in Jesus Christ.

As you read this book, take time to write down your thoughts. Begin to journal your journey to peace and healing. You will be amazed at what the Holy Spirit will reveal to you if you are willing to let Him lead you out of your darkness.

There may be times when you feel alone, possibly abandoned by others. But be encouraged; God has you right where you need to be to receive His blessings. Your life experience was not in vain. Our precious Lord and Savior had a specific plan for your life. Nothing that has happened was a surprise to Him. All of our lives are for His glory and our benefit.

He created us to give Him glory. That includes those of us who are still breathing, as well as those little ones who are now in His loving arms. And the amazing truth is He doesn't waste anything. Nothing is discarded in His eyes. Our trials and mistakes in life are the wheels to drive us into His arms. It is our very lives that He uses as a pathway to help us to see His majesty. His love and forgiveness are so powerful that they cannot be ignored.

# God Spoke to Me

In February 2017, I had an opportunity to attend the Come to the River Women's Retreat in Lake Placid, Florida. Even though I didn't attend the specific host church and had never met these women, I found them to be loving and welcoming. There was a genuine warmth and loving spirit all around; I felt like I had known them all my life. Amazing! There was such a mighty move of God and tender touch of the Holy Spirit. God was truly using these women to minister to me in a way that I had never experienced before. When they announced that they were going to have another retreat in the fall, well, I couldn't resist attending. I signed up and paid in full.

Throughout that year, the Lord repeatedly impressed upon me to write a book. Because I had never written a book before, this notion seemed to be completely out-of-the-box thinking. In my mind, I was clearly no author. But that didn't stop the continual pestering. He would frequently remind me of this new direction, and it became a daily conversation. The dialogue would go something like this: "Really, God? I think You have the wrong person. I'm not equipped to do this, and I don't know what You want me to write about anyway. Surely I must be misunderstanding You." I just couldn't shake it. Surprisingly, there were even times when the topic of writing a book would be mentioned by friends and acquaintances. These comments were completely unsolicited and would appear to have come out of the blue if it hadn't been for the fact that God had been talking to me about it daily.

I prayed for clarity and direction. Then after months of prayer, He reminded me of my earlier experience at the Come to the River retreat and how the atmosphere there had been filled with His Holy Spirit. Surely these women would help me hear from the Lord and would provide me with some answers.

At the Come to the Garden Lake Placid Women's Retreat in October 2017, I had a new purpose for attending. I was focused and determined to understand this new thing God was apparently bringing into my life. I decided to go to this event for two specific reasons: to confirm that what I felt was the prompting of the Holy

Spirit to write a book, and to discover what He wanted me to write about.

Much to my surprise, the confirmation to write the book and the topic on which I was to write were revealed during the Friday night service. That night revealed such a powerful message. The topic was about how God uses the brokenness in the lives of His people to bring about amazing transformation. This included how He uses the broken things that we experience to strengthen our relationship with Him and creates our testimony to help others. He uses our time of doubt and despair to cultivate greater faith and power in our lives.

As the speaker shared, I found myself remembering my past struggles. My mind went back to a time of absolute brokenness, a time when fear and confusion had surrounded and engulfed my heart. It was a season of rebellious choices and selfish desires. It was a time of making desperate decisions to ensure that I could continue to be in control. Although I wasn't consciously aware that this was my underlying objective at the time, my life's desires were all that mattered. I was willing to remove anything or anyone that got in the way of my life's plans, even the life of my firstborn child. My secret sin was conceived. Oh, what a dark time that was! It was the beginning of years of torment.

Then as quickly as those discarded feelings flooded my heart, the Holy Spirit filled my mind with a clear and profound memory of how He totally transformed my life with His healing hand of loving forgiveness. He restored my life. He changed a life that was utterly dying in self-centered rebellion into a life that was alive and gratefully committed to serving others in Christ.

What a revelation! The reminder of my victorious journey took my breath away. It was undoubtedly clear that although this would not have initially been the topic I would have selected, it was absolutely the subject that He wanted me to write about. He wanted to take my profound brokenness and share it with the hurting and the hopeless. He wanted them to see how, when we place our private brokenness in His hands, He can transform our lives. He wanted to show how our lives can become alive with hope and healing and be no longer dead in the trappings of sin. He wanted people to know that they can truly have a life free from guilt and shame, a life filled with strength and healing for His glory. No sin is too great or too horrible. Oh, what a mighty God we serve!

The following day during the morning session, another moving message was given. The topic was about how God repairs our broken vessels in a supernatural way. He doesn't just patch us up; He takes pure gold and pours it between our cracks to seal us and make us whole.

In the Bible, Peter tells us about such victory over suffering. He explains that it is the very trials in our lives that God uses to show that our faith is real. The trial itself purifies us just like fire does gold. The fire (trial) causes the impurities (sin) to come to the top so the Master can remove them. This is what refines the gold (hearts) to the most valuable state. We can rejoice and find hope when we read,

> So be truly glad. There is wonderful joy ahead, even though you have to endure many trials for a little while. These trials will show that your faith is genuine. It is being tested as fire tests and purifies gold—though your faith is far more precious than mere gold. So when your faith remains strong through many trials, it will bring you much praise and glory and honor on the day when Jesus Christ is revealed to the whole world. (1 Peter 1:6–7 NLT)

He takes our tested faith to fortify the broken places in our lives. Our restored lives become of much greater value than before. Remember: God wastes nothing! Even our broken pieces have great value in the potter's hands. When we place our broken vessel in His hands, we become more valuable than the original pottery because our trials have infused us with gold.

At the end of the speaker's message, an altar call was given. She gave an invitation to those who felt that God was calling them to a higher purpose, a new mission or calling in their lives. The Holy Spirit was at work in me for sure. I couldn't recall in recent memory such a pointed, exacting altar call. I felt a distinct prompting of the Holy Spirit to respond. I felt an undeniable holy encouragement, a divine direction to go to the altar. I wanted to follow God and the Holy Spirit. I wanted to pledge my willingness to be obedient to His direction. It was during that altar call that this ministry was birthed.

After a magnificent time with the Lord in the altar, I returned to my seat. It wasn't long afterward that I was overwhelmed by what felt like a personal presence of the Holy Spirit. With incredible authority and clarity, He was speaking directly to me. There, sitting at my table, I had a compelling desire to write what He was saying. It seemed like it needed to be documented. He wanted it to be recorded, and so I opened my notebook, took out my pen, and started to write.

Now, the truth of the matter is that I really wasn't paying much attention to what I was writing. But I knew I had to write down every word I heard in my heart. The voice in my head was clear and distinct. I didn't take time to review sentence structure or spelling. My focus was simply to record what was being revealed. I wrote down every word that He gave me, and when He was done, I closed the notebook.

There was a peaceful excitement that surrounded me. I know that sounds like a contradiction, but honestly, there was such an amazing sensation of resting in His holy presence. It was a sense I had ever known before. Never had I felt His presence or experienced Him like that. This was a time of reverence. It felt like holy worship. This was completely new to me. This was something I had only heard about from others. I had never felt this firsthand. Such power! Such clarity! Such direction! I felt like I had left the physical room and entered a special place, a holy place. What was He doing? How should I respond? I was astounded and amazed. I was rendered speechless.

When our morning session ended, I walked back to my room to rest and try to process all that had taken place in the last eighteen hours. There was so much to take in. I had experienced Him privately before. We had shared intimate moments together in my prayer closet. Those times with Him were always wonderful and a real blessing. But this went far beyond anything I could remember. It wasn't a fleeting encounter. It was an ongoing conversation. Everywhere I walked, I heard His voice.

Later that afternoon, while I was taking an afternoon walk, He proceeded to explain to me how He wanted me to write this book. He impressed upon me the direction I should take. He gave me insights on the spirit I was to convey. Overwhelmed by such precision, I went back to my room, fell on my face, and praised God. I cried, wept, laughed at this magnificent encounter, and thanked Him for His profoundly intimate presence. This was far greater than anything I would have ever imagined.

Shortly before dinner, realizing that I hadn't read what I had written earlier, I opened my notebook and proceeded to read. This is what I wrote.

> Trust Me to lead you. Remember how I speak to you. Guiding you and your thoughts—impressing your senses to align with My thoughts—says the Holy Spirit. Don't rely on your knowledge, but follow your heart, reveal your past, give God your testimony, and let Me, the Holy Spirit, mold it and use it and form it into the ministry I have for you. You were called back in 1970—in Hermansville, Michigan. That call remains and is strengthened by your life's testimony. Don't be mistaken; I have called you. You are to be my ambassador to help Me heal the broken and bring salvation through their

wounding. What the enemy meant for harm, I will use for good. Those children will be the relationship that will bring their parents and loved ones to a deeper relationship with Me. Not to separate them from Me—that is the enemy's lie. I waste nothing! These children are My precious little ones who love and seek Me and desire to love and heal their parents from their pain. Like Jesus, God will use their death to bring their parents into My presence—thus says the Holy Spirit. To be absent from the body is to be present in the Lord. They have been with Us (Trinity) from the moment of their death on earth. We have been loving, nurturing, and enjoying them, preparing them for the day of their reunion. We have helped them see you from Our eyes. Knowing the lies of the enemy that drew you to make the choice you made, knowing about your fears, confusion, and desperation. Also, about your selfishness, rebellion that consumed you when you made your choice. They have had a knowing of your life's journeys that would show you the truth and the new life in Christ, the forgiveness of sins and the redemption of lives, knowing that the power of love far exceeds the influence of evil. The children have had excitement and anticipation for this time when you meet again. They have been praying for you with the Father, asking that you would receive the peace of forgiveness. The children cry for you not out of pain but out of love for you. They have watched you struggle through the rationalization, justification, and denial of what happened that day. They understand those tears you shed when the doctor or nurse said, "Don't worry, honey—the tears are normal. It is a hormonal issue." Or when

> your friend said, "Why are you crying? I thought you wanted to do this." Your child understood that you just didn't know. Some of the children saw that even though you may have done this with the full knowledge that it wasn't a "tissue" and that they were human beings created by God, at that time you still didn't know that the Almighty God designed this to happen. He caught them in their moment and has loved them with a heavenly, holy love because He intended that their lives with Him would be the vehicle He was going to use to bring life and salvation to you. Your child's sacrifice, the cost you paid, brought you to the cross to receive eternal salvation.

Wow! As you can see, it was specific and directed. It clearly was not something that I could have made up. So with this holy message, and with an obedient heart, I am now presenting you this book as He has ordained me to write. I am using His words, His format, and His insight all for one purpose: so you can experience the freedom and the healing forgiveness that is offered to you though Jesus Christ, our Lord and Savior.

May you be blessed, and may you feel the chains fall as you read through these anointed pages and receive the abundant life He has for you.

May you embrace your healing.

# *My Testimony*

## *My Early Years*

Let me tell you a little about myself. I was born on September 29, 1953, into a Midwestern family. I am the third daughter of three girls born to Jacqueline and Fred. I was born in Detroit, Michigan. I carry very few memories of my first four years of life in the city. It was during this time that my mother and father were struggling in their battle with alcoholism. I have heard stories of how Detroit's Finest were on a first-name basis with my mother and father. It wasn't uncommon back then for Daddy to have scratch marks on his face and arms while Mother had bruises. I'm grateful that I don't remember any of that turmoil. I believe my two older sisters had more memories to overcome than I did. My parents found victory when I was four. They became members of Alcoholics Anonymous and never drank again.

For me, my childhood memories began when we moved into a newly developing community on Meadowbrook Lane in Livonia, Michigan. I enjoyed a wonderful childhood in the 1960s. and we lived in a lovely suburban neighborhood. Daddy was finding success in his newfound sobriety and was able to purchase a three-bedroom, one-and-a-half-bath, ranch-style home. This property was a far cry from the cramped, dark duplex we had left in the inner city. In stark contrast, all the homes here were new. They all had beautiful lawns and newly planted trees growing along the sidewalks. Each home was positioned close to each other with only the driveways separating them. We used to refer to this neighborhood as the "house driveway house driveway" development.

My elementary school was only a few blocks away. We were able to walk to school every day in safety. It was there that we learned our letters and numbers. We learned how to play well with others on the playground and master our multiplication tables in the classroom. We learned to develop our minds and imaginations. We were able to freely investigate absolute truths and explore our interests and curiosities. There was free playtime scheduled every day. It was there that we could play pretend and exercise our creativity. My favorite activity was pretending in the playhouse kitchen. This was where I would imagine that I had a husband to cook for and babies to love. We had frilly aprons to wear and pots and pans to wash. How fun that was! We loved and respected our teachers. Our school days began in prayer, followed by the reciting of the Pledge of Allegiance. No metal detectors, no resource officers, no firearms, no drugs. Jackson Elementary School was a place of true learning, loving friendships, and fond memories.

When we came home from school, and on the weekends, we would play outside until the streetlights came on. Our neighborhood was graced with loving people who knew what it meant to be good neighbors. This was long before Mr. Rogers and Sesame Street. We all knew instinctively how to love and care for each other. Every neighbor knew my name, address, and telephone number. While I was playing outside, it was not unusual for someone to call me over for a few freshly baked cookies or a piece of cake. Fresh, cold, homemade lemonade was the beverage of choice in the summer. It seemed like everyone was family. If I misbehaved, well, my parents were only a phone call or short walk away. Everyone seemed to love everyone, and there was a genuine sense of belonging and community.

I enjoyed riding my bike, playing hopscotch, and coloring. We would color on either leftover brown paper grocery bags or special Barbie coloring books Mother would purchase at the local five and dime. Our box of Crayolas had a few broken crayons, but that didn't stop us from creating beautiful masterpieces. Broken crayons still color. Hide-and-seek followed by Red Rover were a couple of the wonderful games we played. We were masters of our universe. We were both free and safe to enjoy life.

There were a few life rules we all had to follow: stay within our neighborhood, be home before the streetlights came on, share with others, and always be kind to one another. These were the basic rules to live by—so simple, easy, and basically profound.

Music and the arts spoke to me from as far back as I can remember. I learned to enjoy classical music and ballet from my parents. In their younger days, Daddy played the French horn in the symphony, and Mother sang opera in college. Their passions for the classics were passed on to me. I would spend countless hours in the basement of our home on my ballet parallel bar, practicing plie and releve moves. I would imagine that I was on stage performing gracefully. My heart was filled with joy. At an early age, around seven, I could lose myself listening to Bach, Mozart, Beethoven, and my favorite, Pyotr Ilyich Tchaikovsky. Many days I would allow myself to enter into that special place. I would carefully open my portable record player, place those treasured vinyl discs on the spindle, and play my 78s. Instantly, the music would transport me into a world of wonder and beauty.

Mother was a stay-at-home mom, though that phrase had not yet been invented. She spent much of her time loving her family and her friends. Mother had a profound impact on my life. Because I was the youngest and she didn't work outside the home, we spent many hours together. She always made me feel special. When I did something that pleased her, I would feel such joy and love. There was a sense of self-fulfillment. She taught me about the joy of giving and doing for others. I remember how often I was made aware of the love she showed others. People would highlight her selfless acts of kindness. Mother was always touched by their comments.

I remember how she would extend herself when it came to my activities in Brownies. She wasn't a den mother but still made an effort to support our troop. Now, she wasn't much of a baker, but she would always make sure I had goodies for our local Brownie meetings. She seemed to delight in helping and supporting me.

One year, she joined the women in our neighborhood and created Christmas stockings for my sister and me. I have that stocking to this day, and it is decorated with all of my childhood interests. There is a little dancing ballerina sewn in the middle representing my love for music and dance. Perfectly positioned in the middle are jewels for my love of jewelry and an artist's palette to remind me of my many Crayola masterpieces. There was, on the center of the stocking's cuff, the Brownie emblem reminding me of those special friendships and activities.

Through her example, I quickly learned how wonderful it felt to please others. I learned that when I pleased others, they seemed to love me more. I began to notice their comments: "You are so kind. You are so thoughtful. You are such a sweet little girl." It left a lasting impression on my heart. Unfortunately, over time the joy of pleasing others mutated into a perverse way to obtain approval and self-worth. It seemed like as long as I was making other people happy, they would love and appreciate me. This approach to life became a hindrance instead of a help. In fact, in many ways it was this overdemanding need to find approval from others that fueled many of my actions later in life. The focus shifted. My desire to please others was slowly overshadowed by the need to get their approval.

Performance-based love. I had totally missed the point. The enemy's deception was cunning. On the outside, everyone saw a kind, giving, and loving little girl. But inside me was a growing and overwhelming need to perform in order to experience love and acceptance. I was totally unaware that God had placed a special spot in my heart that only He could fill. No performance necessary; He had paved the way. Sadly, at that time of my life, I didn't have a personal relationship with Jesus. I only knew *about* God, but I didn't *know* God or His love for me. Over time and left undetected, it overshadowed my motives. It turned out to be a great way to fill that void, that longing for love and acceptance.

I'm sure you've seen homeless individuals on the side of the road holding signs that read, "Will work for food." Well, my sign would have read, "Will work for love." I have since learned that when I give for the purpose of getting, I am no longer a selfless giver; I am a selfish manipulator. Harsh words for sure, but they're true nonetheless. The act of pleasing others became a way for me to receive approval. I learned that if I could control the situation, I would receive love and acceptance. Selfless service, sacrificial love, was replaced by selfish desires and self-managing love. My need to control was born.

My father became an insurance salesman in the city. He continued to be successful and provide for his family. Many of his clients worked during the daytime, and so he frequently conducted his sales calls after hours. He seemed to be gone a lot. I remember missing him in the evenings after dinner. I loved my daddy and wanted to please him too. That was a bit difficult due to his absences. But that made our special times together more special. There were a few exceptional times when he made time for me, and we were able to share special moments together.

One distinct memory was our special times we shared on Sunday mornings. Mother always made sure we were prepared for Sunday church. Back then, little girls wore pretty dresses with white gloves and Mary Jane shoes. She would always have them set out the night before. I loved going to church, and so I was usually up early and ready to go in no time.

It was on these Sunday mornings that Daddy and I would be ready before everyone else. I can still see him sitting in his winged back chair in the corner of the living room. Daddy always wore his dark suit, a white long-sleeved dress shirt, and his signature bolo tie. We would be waiting for my mother and sister to finish getting ready. Waiting was not an activity that I particularly cared for. Impatience was a common struggle in my life back then. I was always on the go, always having to do something. Most of the time, I filled that time of impatience with incessant, unnecessary talking—jabber, jabber, jabber. Sunday mornings were no exception. In fact, I think it was one of my best times to exhibit such nonsense. Daddy knew that. He would remind me that I needed to settle down. Daddy would say, "Neva Ann, make sure your mind is in gear before you put your mouth into motion." His comment would be followed by a brief chuckle. Then he would gently pat his knee, motioning for me to come over and sit on his lap. That was my signal: our special time was to begin.

I would get the Sunday funny papers section of the *Detroit Free Press*. There was an inviting and compassionate smile on my father's face. I truly believe he looked forward to our special Sunday morning time together too. I would climb up onto his lap; there was always plenty of room for me. I felt safe and secure in his lap. His arm held me close so that I didn't fall. He would open the newspaper with a flamboyant gesture. The paper would fly and snap in the air as he opened it. Then with a smile on his face, he would proceed to read the comic strips. Oh, how I loved sitting on his lap and listening to him read aloud. He would read with such expression, like he was each character. We would chuckle together at *Family Circle* and *Blondie. Beetle Bailey* was his favorite; *Charlie Brown* was mine. It was a wonderful, loving, and safe place. I can still smell his aftershave, Old Spice. Life felt safe, simple, and serene. I didn't have to perform or make him love me during these moments. His love for me seemed to flow without any help from me. My life was filled with friends, family, and faith. They all seemed interwoven in our Midwestern, suburban life. Classmates, neighbors, ballet recitals, Sunday school songs, Bible stories on felt boards, and Brownie Troop outings—it was truly a wonderful life.

But that was soon to change. My life was about to be shaken at the very core. I was around eight years old and attending third grade. Four years into their sobriety, my father and mother began having arguments. It didn't seem like much at first, but as time went on, they became more and more argumentative. My daddy began to sleep in the other bedroom. I didn't really understand why, but we were to leave Daddy alone when he was resting in his bedroom.

Then one Saturday afternoon, my mother took me to the nearby park and informed me that they were going to have a divorce. Now, back then divorce was not very common. If you happened to know anyone who had a divorce, they were frowned upon. I remember there was a family in our neighborhood who got a divorce, and everyone talked about how sad they were for them and their children. All I remembered was that they were the divorced family, and my friend didn't come out and play like she used to. She would be away from home for periods of time. It seemed so mysterious. I wasn't really sure what it all meant, but I knew by the way she spoke that it wasn't good.

Mother told me that we were going to have to move to a new home. She said that I was going to attend a different school but that I didn't need to worry; Mommy and Daddy still loved me. It was all so confusing. All I had ever really known was my wonderful life on Meadowbrook Lane and my friends at Jackson Elementary. Anything else was going to be strange and unfamiliar. No, I wasn't happy about the news.

This was the first time I remember experiencing the feeling of not being secure or in control. I began to fear that no matter how nice or giving I was, this divorce thing was going to change the course of my life. I couldn't stop it from happening. This was altogether foreign to me, and I didn't like it.

Within a week, we were all packed up and moving to a two-bedroom duplex across town. My new school was in an established neighborhood. It was an old, two-story brick building. The classrooms smelled of disinfectant with an underlying odor of mildew. The hallways were dark, and everyone seemed unhappy and preoccupied. I don't remember any bright colors or flowers. All I remember were tall, dark trees outside and echoing hallways dotted with rusting drinking fountains. There wasn't any joy in people's steps. My classmates were not interested in the new girl. I spent most of my time alone. Lunch time in the cafeteria was the worst. I remember sitting by myself, and when someone did come by to sit next to me, it was only because there was nowhere else to sit or they had other friends joining them. They made it clear they were not sitting there for my sake!

Daddy would come and visit on weekends. Our visits seemed strange; it was like he was a friend of the family instead of my daddy.

My parents spent time on the phone arguing. Even though we didn't live together, they were still unhappy with each other. Sometimes I could hear Mother's voice from the other room. She seemed to cry a lot back then, and so being home wasn't much fun. It by no means gave me any relief from my experience during those long days at school.

I spent a lot of my free time walking to the nearby park. The park was only a couple of blocks away. It didn't have any trees, as I recall, but the fields were full of weeds. There was an old basketball court at the far end of the property. The hoop, which was constructed from dirty and rusted chains, was positioned on top of a corroded metal pole. As dreary as it all seemed, this was a time I could call my own. I felt so sad and out of control when I was home. I was unsure of everything. I thought I had to find a way to feel safe, secure, and happy again.

During my walks, I would try to understand what was going on. For an eight-year-old who was used to pleasant neighborhoods, friends, and lunchtimes, all this was daunting. Trying to make sense of this was extremely difficult. My imagination would turn to things that I could grasp. I had recently watched the movie *The Wizard of Oz*. Maybe this was a test to see if I could stay happy in a scary place. Dorothy was always trying to keep the Scarecrow, Lion, and Tin Man encouraged. Maybe that was what I was supposed to be doing, keeping everyone happy and encouraged. But how could I do that when I felt so unhappy? We had stopped going to church, but I still remembered some of those stories. Maybe this was like the story I had heard about Joseph. I remembered the characters my Sunday school teacher had placed on the felt boards. He was always being treated badly. Even his own brothers hated him. He had a lot of reasons to be discouraged, but he kept on believing that God would take care of him—and God did! God even made him like a king!

But that God seemed far away. I couldn't see how He could make anyone royalty in this place. I was sure He would not like this place anyway. I really didn't think He would want to be here.

It all seemed so dark and depressing. There were no pretty dresses, white gloves, or felt storyboards. I surely didn't see me as a queen! Nevertheless, I still attempted to talk to Him on my walks. I would ask Him why this had all happened. I wanted Him to make things to go back to the way they had used to be. I wanted to go back to playing with my friends, riding my bike, dancing in the basement with my record player, and sitting on my daddy's lap reading *Beetle Bailey*. I wanted my mommy and daddy to love each other again and stop fighting. I wanted to go back to Meadowbrook Lane. God had to fix this! He was my only hope. *Where are You, God?* That desperate time seemed like a lifetime away, like it was someone else's life. Time seemed to drag on.

Over the next few months, I tried to adjust to this strange life. I really struggled to settle in. I didn't make very many new friends. I was falling behind in my schoolwork, but Mother was sure that summer school would bring it all back in line.

I'm not sure how it happened, but one day I noticed that it seemed like mother was smiling more each day. Maybe she was having an easier time adjusting. Mother always seemed in control back then, except for the times I would hear her cry in her bedroom. She seemed to always have answers to my questions. What was her secret? How could she be getting happier and I was getting sadder? I began to notice that when Mother and Daddy spoke on the phone, they didn't seem to be yelling as much. There were even times when I thought Mother was enjoying the conversation. They started to spend more time together—not just talking on the phone, but going out together. They seemed to be happy together. They didn't fight and yell. In fact, there were times when I saw them together laughing and holding hands. They didn't seem to be mad at each other anymore. Much to my surprise and delight, one evening Mother sat my sister and me down and asked us if we would like to move back in with Daddy. My sister's only concern was whether we would be able to keep our dog. I simply wanted to go back to the life I knew and loved so well at Meadowbrook Lane. Did I want to move back? Of course I did! How did this happen? Did God hear me after all? Did He really answer my prayers? I would later come to understand that my parents had come to a point in their early sobriety when they began to realize they had never known each other sober. They didn't know whether they loved the sober versions of each other. Once they had a chance to discover their sober selves, they were able to see that they did in fact love each other.

And with that, we were planning a wedding for my parents. That always seemed funny to me—planning a wedding for my mom and dad. No one else in my class had experienced their parents' wedding. It seemed that as quickly as the decision to move out was made, the decision was made to move back in. By that fall, we were living on Meadowbrook Lane and my life was back to normal. How wonderful this was. Looking back, even though the time away from Meadowbrook Lane seemed like a lifetime, in reality we were away for less than a year. Jackson Elementary and fourth grade, here I come.

We enjoyed our family time again, but this time I think I valued it more than before. Before the divorce, I never thought that our lives could ever change, but I was wrong. Life is always changing and evolving into new adventures and experiences, some good and some not so good. I learned that I needed to learn how to enjoy what I could, when I could. I discovered sometimes people will do things you don't expect, but you have to still try to trust in what you know to be true. I had to figure things out for myself. One of my deductions was even though I didn't know where God was when I was scared, if I prayed to God, He would eventually answer my prayers. Like my Sunday school teacher taught me through song, "Jesus loves me, this I know, for the Bible tells me so." Jesus was my friend, and He loved me and was listening to my prayers. He was at my beck and call. If I stayed a good girl, He would answer my prayers sooner or later. I saw Him as a heavenly Santa Claus, if you will.

For the following four years, life on Meadowbrook Lane moved along uneventfully. Gratefully, I no longer had to deal with the isolation of sitting alone in the cafeteria or walking to dreary parks for entertainment. Wonderfully, friends, school, and church became my life's experiences once again. My friends eagerly welcomed me back, but the divorced family and my friend had moved away by the time we returned. I frequently wondered if she was enduring the heartache of divorce and separation from her friends like I had. I prayed for her for months. I would ask Jesus to bring her family back together. To my knowledge, He didn't.

I was in eighth grade when my father started to experience some health issues. As he became more and more successful, the pressures of his work began to take their toll. It was suggested that he find a place where he could go to slow down and reduce his stress. The city was no place for rest or stress reduction. By now, our little community had grown into a sprawling suburb. Everything was changing. What was once a beautiful field or flourishing forest was now a shopping mall or new subdivision. Another change was on the horizon.

## The Farm

During Easter vacation that year, we took a trip to the northern part of our state. My parents were aware of the beauty and tranquility this remote location could offer. We didn't go on many vacations back then. Daddy was always working, so given idea that we were going on a vacation, driving for miles, and staying in motels, the excitement was overwhelming. My sister and I thought this was going to be a wonderful, educational, sightseeing vacation to see beautiful waterfalls, majestic forests, and natural wildlife. We were completely unaware that it was going to be a trip to explore relocation possibilities.

During our travels, Mother and Daddy found a local newspaper and began looking at property listings. It wasn't long before they found a beautiful farmhouse for sale. It was located in a small town of about four hundred people. They thought this could be exactly what they were looking for. No traffic, no hustle or bustle, just a beautiful farmhouse with acres of stunning open pasture land in a rural farming community. Just what the doctor ordered. Tucked in the middle of our sightseeing excursions, they scheduled an appointment with a local realtor. The farm was situated in a very remote location. They drove for miles. It took forty-five minutes to drive to this isolated location. As we drove, we would see only an occasional home or farm dot the landscape, but nothing of any metropolitan influence. The property was quite a distance from the closest city, and it was nothing like back home. At least downstate, there were towns between cities. There were gas stations on every corner, grocery stores in every block, and shopping malls and clothing stores in between. That was clearly not the case here. I remember driving up to the property, which was situated on top of a hill. You could see it from miles away. There sat a humble, white, two-story farmhouse nestled behind two overgrown evergreen trees. One could see acres of farmland, a beautiful apple orchard, cinder block, two-car garage, two red toolsheds, and a neat, whitewashed horse corral—all located on the forty-acre homestead. But by far the massive, double red dairy barn was the most eye-catching structure. It stood majestically as if to announce the generations of families that had loved and farmed this land.

I had never considered farm life. I was a city girl through and through. The TV comedy *Green Acres* came to mind. My sister, however, was all but overcome with excitement. She had a love for nature. She loved dogs, horses, and the outdoors. She instantly saw the wondrous possibilities. I was a bit more skeptical, but I had to concede there seemed to be something peaceful about this place. Mother inspected the house, and Daddy surveyed the barn and the grounds. My sister and I checked out the barn. It smelled of cow manure and hay. She was delighted. I was not.

We all walked the property lines. This was a 120-acre farm. Forty homestead acres; forty hay fields, with six head of grazing, white-faced Hereford cows; and forty acres of evergreen trees. It was nothing like our home downstate. As far as animals were concerned, we only had a stray dog, and she was a handful. I couldn't imagine tending to cows. Cutting the grass on Meadowbrook Lane was always a chore. How were we going to handle forty acres of hay? Across the road was the forty-acre parcel with evergreen trees—Christmas trees that we could sell each year in Chicago. No, this was way too different. I was sure we would not be seriously considering this farm as a place for Daddy to rest.

Much to my surprise, my parents agreed to purchase the property right then and there! They signed papers before we returned home and said we would be able to move in at the end of the school year.

How could that be? Nothing made sense. We spent the rest of our vacation talking about all the wonders and possibilities that this new home could offer. Daddy said we could have horses. That thrilled my sister. Mother explained how fun it would be to freshen up the home. She said I could pick out my own wallpaper and be in charge of decorating my bedroom. I have to admit, the thought of being in charge of decorating my room sounded fun. I had never been put in charge of anything like that. This may be okay after all. I was somewhat excited about the possibility of a new adventure, but time would tell.

By the time we returned home, I had convinced myself that this move was not for me. I didn't want to leave the life I had grown to love and trust. Mixed emotions filled my heart. For the second time, I had really begun to feel like I was not completely in control of my life. Circumstances and other people's decisions were once again taking me to unexpected places. My personal desires didn't seem to play into any of the plans that were being made. Decorating a room on farm was nothing compared to living in the city where I knew everyone and understood all the rules. The rules! What about the rules? There weren't even any street lights at the farm. I felt vulnerable and unsure. I didn't like that feeling at all. It reminded me of those early months during Mom and Dad's divorce. *Maybe all I have to do is ask God to give me what I want again and everything will turn out,* I reasoned.

Over the next few months, as we were finishing out our school year, Mother tried to ease my concerns. She would remind me that this was going to be good for our family. She reasoned that I needed to grow up and to start thinking more of others instead of myself. She repeatedly said, "Neva, the world is not going to revolve around you all the time." I'm not sure I wanted the world to revolve around me; I simply didn't want to leave my familiar surroundings. Mother reinforced the importance of the fact that this was going to help Daddy's health. One of her new sayings was, "Neva, remember, you are only one, and there are four of us." I tried to adopt that line of thinking. In my immature way of thinking, all I heard was that I wasn't important anymore. I wanted to please her, but the thought that I wasn't important anymore really hurt my feelings.

Later that summer, we packed up all our belongings into hastily marked cardboard boxes. We wrapped our precious items in newspaper. Our furniture was loaded onto a big moving truck. This was probably the largest truck I had ever seen in our neighborhood. It was the kind of moving truck that moved families across the country. Believe me, it felt like we were moving to the other side of the continent, not just up north. We said our goodbyes to our friends, our family, our community, and what seemed to be my life. We drove over five hundred miles and moved onto this 120-acre farm in the Upper Peninsula of Michigan. How difficult this was for me. Everything I knew changed. My life would never be the same. *Things are moving too quickly. I have to get control of my life,* I thought. God didn't seem to hear me. *Why, God?*

The town we moved to was very different from our "house driveway house driveway" subdivision. It had unpaved roads, sprawling farmland, and homes on large parcels of land. People referred to them as forties. That was because most land was divided up into parcels of forty-acre lots. We had three of these forties. Downtown consisted of a post office, general store, movie theater, butcher shop, motel, funeral home, gas station, the Big R restaurant, the Hut (which was a local student hangout), a bar, and the two-story public school that housed grades kindergarten through twelfth. Oh, and I can't forget the one blinking stoplight.

It was a challenge adjusting to such a small farming town, to say the least. Making new friends was not easy for me when I was in third grade, and it wasn't any easier in my freshman year of high school. I was seen as the girl from the big city. People didn't really care for those of us from downstate; we were seen as outsiders. Looking back, I think much of that was probably warranted to some degree. We tended to be on a faster track than this quiet, laid-back, rural township. The community I came from was characterized by subdivisions, cement roads, traffic lights, and constant activity. My new community was portrayed as quiet and easygoing, with one traffic light. And believe me, there was little traffic, to be sure.

High school was primarily uneventful. There were the occasional sports victories and community events, but nothing that would be seen as globally earth shattering. I was not particularly popular, though I tried desperately to be. Learning the new ways and the community traditions was difficult and confusing. How would I ever fit in? Did the rules from my old neighborhood still apply? (1) Stay within our neighborhood. Well, there were no neighborhoods, per se. Most homes were defined as forties or property. (2) Be home before the street lights came on. Well, that is a tough one as well. As mentioned before, there were no streetlights. (3) Share with others and always be kind to one another. Now that one could easily apply. But it was still an adjustment. You see, here people were nice, but they had already established whom they shared with. I was still the outsider and had no history with these people. I found it hard to share my past experiences. My life downstate was so different. I had plenty of history with Meadowbrook Lane people, just not the farming people. To make matters even more troubling, my life's experiences didn't include sharing with people who didn't know me, and so I found it hard to always be kind when I felt so out of place.

Maybe I needed to discover their rules. But what were their new rules? It seemed like I had to start all over. I was beginning to feel like I was losing a grip on life. I spent many nights crying and praying that God, my heavenly Santa Claus, would help me. Maybe He could send me a friend, someone who could help me navigate in this new location. I really wanted to find someone who would accept me even though I was from downstate. It would be someone whom I could relate with, laugh with, and confide in. So much was going on. Everything was changing. I didn't want to go through this all alone. I looked around me and saw that everyone had been friends all their lives, but like I said, I was not a part of their history.

It was in this time of trying to fit in, to find that special friend, that God did answer my prayer. He blessed me with someone who seemed to understand me like no other. Linda was a native of this small town. She knew and loved everyone, and everyone loved her. She was loving and accepting of others and always found the best in people. She was very shy back then and was also looking and praying for that special friend. The day we met, we knew this was the friendship we were both praying for. We instantly became best friends—kindred spirits, if you will. She was closer to me than my own sister. Linda was family. We would spend hours talking about God, life, boys, and what we should wear to school the next day. We sat next to each other in the cafeteria and study hall. We spent countless hours in my room listening to records and sharing secrets. We took typing together and enjoyed Mr. Rodman's science class. In the summers, we worked at the same restaurant as waitresses. We learned about customer service and self-reliance. The Me Too movement was decades away, but we could have added our names to that list. Navigating around the freezer when the owner was in the area—now, that could be tricky! We always made a point of having each other's backs. No real harm done, just another one of life's experiences we lived through together.

We talked about our dreams and shared hopes for the future. We could always be found on Friday nights at the VFW Legion Hall, where we danced to live music. Local bands would come and play all the current rock and roll music. We would laugh and dance until we were exhausted. Sometimes during a break, we would hide in the bathroom and sneak a cigarette or two. I wasn't much of a risk taker back then, but I had my moments. Together we seemed to be able to face life with courage and strength. Linda always had a word of encouragement, and I had words of wisdom. What a team we were! She became a lifelong friend. To this day, we share an exceptional relationship of understanding and unconditional love for each other.

As time passed, life became easier on the farm. We truly enjoyed the benefits of that rural community. People not only knew everyone, but they had a genuine love and concern for each other. Also, they were all related to each other in some way. It was a great place to practice one of my mother's favorite sayings: "If you don't have something nice to say, don't say anything at all." That came in handy when you discovered you were talking about someone's cousin! Needless to say, the consequences of not following such wisdom could be disastrous.'

## My Encounter with Jesus

Our family attended a very small Methodist church in the neighboring town of Hermansville, Michigan. We had about fifty members. The church had beautiful oak pews (no cushions), stained-glass windows, and hardwood floors. The structure was simple and could remind one of an old church, possibly built in the late 1800s. The bright yellow paint that covered the exterior made it stand out. People could see our church for miles. I loved seeing our church friends every Sunday. We would sing songs of the ages out of old hymnals. The sopranos seemed to relish the opportunity to reach for the high notes. The basses loved to give us the deep rich sound of the lower notes. I loved going to that church.

Our pastor was considered young for his vocation. I'm sure

that was what contributed to his sermons always being given with such enthusiasm and passion. The messages were clear and consistent. They all spoke of living a good life and stated that Jesus loved us. I don't remember much focus on the topic of sin. There seemed to be a consistent theme of living a good life and loving one another. If we followed the rules, stayed strong, and made good decisions, we would be fine. This doctrine seemed reasonable to me. I adopted the thought that all I had to do was rely on my resources and understanding of what was right and wrong, and I would be successful in God's eyes. How wonderful! Little did I know, however, that this early misinterpretation would begin a life's trajectory of greater self-reliance and rebellion toward God. My life's theme became, "Don't worry, God. I've got this."

It was in this church that during the spring of my junior year, I had a face-to-face encounter with God. It was during the Easter season. Nothing appeared to be out of the ordinary; everyone attended and was seated in the usual places. All the elements of the service were in place: opening hymns, reading of Scripture, passing the collection plate, and more singing, followed by the sermon. As the service progressed, I became aware of a change in the room. I sensed a captivating countenance in the atmosphere. During the offering time, while everyone had their heads bowed in prayer, I looked up at the window where the small choir of dedicated members sang each week. There He was! I saw what appeared to be a male figure in a white robe with His hands extended out toward me. My impression was that it was Jesus Himself. Oh, how beautifully radiant He was! It appeared to me like He was beckoning me to follow him. Love and peace surrounded me. Tears welled up inside me. The church was filled with His radiance. All else around me seemed to vanish. At that moment, it was just Jesus and me. I sat there basking in His warm embrace. While I continued to see Him by the window, I could feel His touch all around me and through me. What an amazing moment—one I will never forget!

Now, I don't ever remember the pastor giving an altar call for salvation. No petition to come forward in response to his message. No call to make a decision for Christ. That wasn't something this church did, so to think I was being called would never have entered my mind. I wasn't sure why I saw what I did. I didn't know what the purpose was for such a magnificent vision. Nevertheless, I absolutely knew that what I saw was real. But I was unsure of what to make of it. It was something that needed explanation for sure.

I considered sharing this with Linda. There were times when we would talk about God. Linda and I were of different faiths, and so our conversations were often about the general existence of God. We would share how much we loved God and that He loved us. We wrestled with our limited understanding of morality. The Vietnam War was raging, and certainly God would watch over our friends. There were plenty of opportunities to call upon Him in our teenaged lives, trying to navigate relationships and exams. But we never interfered with each other's religious upbringings. It was abstract and spiritual, but never religious. That aspect of God was left to our individual church pastors and priests. In my mind, this experience was more in the church teaching arena and outside the realm of general spiritual discussion. It was too bizarre to comprehend without additional theological input. At least for now, I needed to wait to share it with her. I needed to get a better handle on what it really was.

Mother was the most likely candidate with whom to reveal this celestial encounter. She would hopefully understand and shed some light on it. Since moving to the farm, we had continued to have a wonderfully close relationship, but we were both experiencing a time of transition; mine was growing into a young adult, and hers was adjusting to farm life. There were times when we didn't enjoy the easygoing relationship we'd had back on Meadowbrook Lane. Like most mother-daughter relationships at that age, we didn't always see eye to eye. I really wasn't sure if this would be one of those times. Now, don't get me wrong, we would talk about God and His mighty power. Mother believed in God's healing miracles. Something like this may make sense to her, I thought. Even so, I was still a bit nervous to share this holy phenomenon with her. I knew it was real, and I didn't want to risk someone stealing it away by telling me it was just my imagination. I hoped that her knowledge of our faith and her experience of God would enable her to explain this confusing experience.

Mother was always willing to listen to me. Even when my ideas may have seemed a bit unbelievable, she would still indulge me. It was not uncommon for me to burst into the kitchen before breakfast and share the previous night's dream. She would always have some words of wisdom on what it meant. I hoped that she might be open to this as well. However, this revelation was far more important than a random dream. I cautiously asked her if I could talk with her alone about something important. I didn't want my dad or sister to overhear our discussion; it would be too risky. I was afraid that it could possibly open up a group discussion. I really wasn't ready for that.

Later that night, after Daddy went outside to check on the cows and my sister was out with her horse, Mother and I found a quiet place in the living room to talk. I privately shared my vision, and she listened intently. She was interested in my story and seemed intrigued. She sat patiently with compassion in her eyes. I tried to be as specific as I could. I didn't want to overlook any detail. Where He appeared, how He looked, what I felt, what He seemed to convey—all needed to be revealed. Mother had always embraced the reality of Jesus, but this was something new. This was something she had never personally experienced. To my dismay, Mother couldn't explain it. It was beyond her experience, knowledge, or spiritual insight. She felt that only a religious scholar, someone with theological training, would be able to enlighten us on the meaning of such a profoundly divine experience. She suggested I share it with our pastor. Maybe he could reveal the meaning of this.

Mother's advice could be trusted. She always seemed to know best, though I was still very nervous about exposing such an intimate experience with someone I didn't really know. Other than seeing him on Sunday mornings and at an occasional wedding or funeral, I didn't have much of a relationship with our pastor. He was always pleasant enough. He conveyed confidence in his knowledge of the church and church doctrine. Maybe he was the right person to explain this after all. I reluctantly agreed to talk with him.

I scheduled an appointment to meet with my pastor the following week. We started our meeting with a light conversation about school and our church events. This was followed by a pleasant prayer thanking God for His provisions and asking Him to guide our conversation. That helped set the atmosphere. I'm not sure what He thought we were going to discuss, but he seemed willing to engage in whatever topic I was going to bring. I was still unsure and nervous. *Where do I start? How do I begin?* I began by telling him that I always loved Jesus and that I loved God. I told him that I was familiar with prayer and had felt a special closeness to God ever since my childhood experience of God's answered prayer. My pastor needed to realize that I was a good girl, that I was always trying to follow the rules and make right decisions. After a brief pause, I took a deep breath and began. I tried the best I could to explain what I saw. I needed him to know that I was sure that this was a real encounter with Jesus. I described how He looked in front of the stained-glass windows. How the atmosphere changed when Jesus appeared. How Jesus seemed to be asking me to follow Him. I shared with the pastor that I felt like Jesus was inviting me to come with Him. I felt like He wanted me to do something important. I didn't know what it was that Jesus wanted me to do, but I knew He wanted me to embrace Him in a new way. It was vitally important that the pastor understood that this wasn't something I had just made up. He needed to know that this was totally unexpected and unsolicited. I desperately needed him to grasp the reality of my encounter with Jesus. I needed him to help me understand it.

He listened intently. After a few moments of silent reflection, he said that he was glad that I had had this wonderfully spiritual experience. He told me that it was nice and clearly a special moment in my life. Then he finished by telling me that I should spend more time reading my Bible and praying. That was it! Nice. Read my Bible and pray? No revelation, no inspirational comment, no theological explanation given. I was speechless!

I don't believe he truly understood what had happened that night with Jesus and me. His response left me dumbfounded. I knew whom I had seen, but still didn't know why or what I was to do. Even still, it left me with a profound desire to serve and follow Christ in a meaningful way. I might not have understood the depth of what had occurred or exactly what I was to do next, but I did believe that it gave me a newfound power and purpose. With that in mind, I began exploring the possibility of a career serving Christ.

It was 1970, during the peak of the "Jesus freak" era. Young people were finding Jesus in droves. They were preaching on the street corners, starting Christian youth groups on campuses, and sharing the gospel in theaters. Billy Graham Crusades were in full swing. *Jesus Christ Superstar* was on Broadway; the soundtrack could be heard on the radio every day. There was an overwhelming excitement around Jesus. One could hear about Him in churches, coliseums, on radios, and in theaters.

I had always enjoyed the arts and theater. In fact, earlier in the year, I had performed the lead part in the school play, *The Groom Said No.* It had been a comedy, and I had had a blast. Could it be that I could combine my love for the theater and Jesus into a career? Serving Christ through drama would blend my personal desires of theater and the arts with my newfound vision of Jesus. It would be a perfect fit.

Motivated by this purpose and energized by the adventure it would hold, I spent the next few months applying to colleges that had good drama departments with a Christian environment. Unfortunately, there weren't any colleges nearby that would meet both the drama and Christian criteria. I would have to find something out of the area—away from home.

At first, the thought of leaving home seemed daunting. Another move to a strange place where I didn't know anyone initially didn't sound appealing. I had just gone through that. Then I realized that although it was a somewhat unpleasant experience, I had learned how to do it and, quite frankly, come through it very well. I now had new friends and wonderful experiences that would never have been possible if I had stayed on Meadowbrook Lane. Nevertheless, I didn't want to spend the rest of my life on the farm. In my heart, I knew I was a city girl after all. Therefore I began to concentrate on the possibilities of a career away from the farm. If I was going to pursue a career in the theater, I had better opportunities downstate.

It wasn't long before my apprehension left. The thrill I had experienced on stage, coupled with the feelings I had for Jesus, began to grow. I felt so empowered, so grown-up, so unshakable. I was sure God would provide whatever I needed, especially because He was going to be part of this adventure. To pursue a career in the arts was beyond anything I could have imagined. I had a strategy, and I was going to do everything in my power to execute it. I couldn't let the fear of being alone, living without my family, deter me. I knew that if I continued to make good decisions, follow the rules, and stay in control, all would work out. At least it had seemed to work so far. "Don't worry, God. I've got this."

## My College Experience

In the spring of my senior year, I was accepted to a Methodist theological liberal arts college and proceeded to pursue an education in drama and communications. The college was over five hundred miles from our farm. This was going to be the first time I was without my family. I thought I was so grown-up and independent; my time had come. This time the move would be my choice, my decision, and solely for my benefit!

I don't remember the specific scheduling conflict, but my

parents were not able to drive me to college. They did, however, have a friend who was going to be traveling in the general direction of my college campus. He agreed to let me hitch a ride with him. I arrived on campus early, a day before any of the other students. We didn't realize that the dorms were not accepting new students until Sunday. We arrived Saturday with suitcase and trunk in hand. The dorm mother agreed to make an exception and invited me in. The fact that my ride was not staying and I didn't have anywhere else to stay played a big part in her generous offer. The only person in my entire dorm was the RA, and she was busy getting ready for the onslaught of students that was to arrive the next day. I spent the first couple of hours busying myself by unpacking my suitcase and trunk. I toured the dorm and got somewhat familiar with my new surroundings. I found the student union, student office, and chapel. There was a small, family-owned hamburger stand a couple of blocks off campus. There were no McDonald's locations in this small college town back then. I ventured out and had my first meal on my own. I was still a bit insecure, but I was sure I could overcome the jitters I was feeling. Just stick to the plan!

After my meal, I walked back to campus. It was later in the afternoon. Evening was beginning to settle in. The campus seemed quiet and somewhat isolated from the small college town. I noticed that there were large trees and beautiful landscaping in front of my dorm. The other campus buildings were all brick and now seemed somewhat stoic. As night set, the campus no longer felt inviting. I began to feel the chill of this educational institution. The excitement of a new chapter of my life was fading.

When I finished exploring my new surroundings, it happened. I was overcome by a profound sense of being alone, and it absolutely seized me. I had never felt such isolation, such loneliness. The silence in my room was deafening. Where did this come from? How did this happen? I thought I had it all together and planned out. This wasn't part of any of my anticipated adventure.

We didn't have the internet or cell phones back then. I couldn't pick up my phone and call or text someone. All telecommunication was connected by landline. The call would be considered a long-distance call and would involve the services of an operator. The call would have expensive rates. The only money I had was what I had saved up from my summer waitress job. That money was to be used for personal items, not long-distance phone calls.

The first night alone was horrible. All I seemed to do was cry. I didn't think I would ever stop. I didn't know anyone, and nothing was familiar. No Mom, no Dad, no Linda. Even the thought of God seemed distant. There was a real sense of abandonment. Had I made a mistake? Was I just fooling myself? I began to question this plan of mine. This was supposed to be more fun. This was supposed to be easier. The reality of being independent became clear to me. It was evident that if I was going to survive this experience, I had to get hold of myself, by myself. I remembered the lessons I had learned in my little church: if we followed the rules, stayed strong, and made good decisions, we would be fine. So I embraced my life's mantra once again: "Don't worry, God. I've got this."

The next day, students from all over the country began to arrive. The excitement of the new school year filled the air. Cars continually pulled up at the curb. Fathers were unloading suitcases and trunks, and mothers and students were investigating dorm rooms and amenities. I remember being struck by the fact that so many other students' parents were sharing this first day college experience. My heart ached for mine. *Focus, Neva. You have a plan!*

I met my roommate around lunchtime. I helped her settle in, and then we were off to the Student Union for a bite to eat. She was so different from any of my friends back home. The first thing I noticed about her was her big, thick, curly auburn hair—frizzy, if you will. It seemed to overtake her. She was simply dressed and had a constant smile on her face. She had the kind of smile that could be described as beaming. But the most notable characteristic was that she didn't seem to stop talking, and she didn't seem to have a wide range of topics to chat about. All she could talk about was Jesus. Now, don't get me wrong, I loved Jesus. I knew all about Jesus. At least, I knew about the Jesus I had heard about on those felt storyboards back in Sunday school. I knew about the Jesus I had experienced during that amazing encounter last year. But she seemed to be taking this Jesus thing to a totally different level. I didn't understand the kind of enthusiasm and zeal that she had for Christ. It simply seemed a bit over the top for me. She seemed to have inside knowledge. This privileged understanding was something that I knew nothing about. It was a bit intimidating, quite frankly. She told me about a group that she was going to be involved in. She said it was a group of students that met on campus three nights a week. They were going to spend an hour and a half reading Scripture, worshiping in song, and praying to Jesus. She asked if I wanted to come with her that night. It was going to be the first meeting of the semester, and it would be great! I passed. It seemed a bit much. It felt too radical. As I look back at this time of my life, I find it amazing how quickly the idea of studying God's Word and being in His presence became an object of intimidation instead of intrigue.

Not surprisingly, I fit into the theater group easily. We all had the same interests, and some had real talent. We were all very creative, artistic, and full of life. There was a sense of excitement when I was around them. We would act out scenes from movies or famous authors' and literary playwrights' works at the drop of a hat. Improvisation was common. Tennessee Williams was a favorite. My drama classes were the highlight of my time away from home.

In fact, as time went on, home became a distant thought. The memory of my divine encounter seemed to fade as well. I attended the mandatory Wednesday morning chapel services. I even joined the campus choir. But my time was not spent enriching my experience with God or even reviewing my elementary understanding of Jesus. I tried to keep myself busy by following the rules, staying strong, and making good decisions.

During my freshman year, I began to spend more and more of my time in party mode. This wouldn't have been placed in the making good decisions category, but the allure of independence and acceptance was overwhelming to me. I thought I was mastering the ability to take control of my life.

Living life on my terms was becoming easier as the days went on. This newfound independence, freedom, and popularity overshadowed my original strategy. My life took on new rules. Those rules instructed me to enjoy life and not worry. It didn't take long before my activities and friends surrounded me in a world of drinking, boys, and worldly excitement—which led to poor grades, drunken parties, hangovers, and date rape. My life was in a downward spiral. How quickly it all became out of control.

When my parents heard about my drinking escapades and the resulting date rape, they drove downstate to help me. Their focus was on getting me help concerning my drinking. Their opinion of the date rape was that it wouldn't have happened if I hadn't been drinking. Although there was no evidence of typical alcoholism behavior, not surprisingly they were only focused on the drinking. They were fearful that I might be following in their footsteps. After a week of counseling, I returned to school, vowing not to drink again. I would get my life back in order. Alcoholic or not, I would attend AA meetings. That would fix everything.

By this time, my roommate had convinced me that I didn't know Jesus like I should. I began to think that my encounter and divinely inspired purpose might have been a misunderstanding after all. I really didn't want to tell people about my encounter with Jesus. My newfound friends didn't seem to want to hear about Him. Frankly, I was beginning to think that maybe Jesus didn't like me anymore either. At least, the Jesus my roommate knew and spoke about didn't approve of me or endorse what I was doing. She made it clear to me that she certainly didn't. But how could that be? I thought I was making good decisions, taking care of myself, and enjoying life. The thought that Jesus didn't like me really didn't make sense. Let's face it: I was at this school because of Him.

All of this became too confusing, and I couldn't make sense of it all. I convinced myself that life was too short to dwell on something that was probably beyond man's general understanding anyway. I decided that I simply didn't need to spend time thinking about or discussing it. If the topic of Jesus came up, I politely got up and excused myself. I did not want to feel rejected by a God whom I didn't really know and who must not really know me.

As I look back on this period of my life, I am reminded that there is a significant difference between knowing about God and knowing God. Once we embrace a personal relationship with Him and seek to follow Him, the desires of our hearts change in magnificent ways. The longing to be with and to rest in His arms is overwhelming. The need for spiritual nourishment is compelling. But the need to be in control of my own life would overshadow me and prevent me from seeking Him. It wouldn't be for several more years before this life-changing truth would become real and redeem my life. In the meantime, "Don't worry, God. I've got this."

## After College

I met my first husband later that year. I didn't talk much about God or Jesus with him; it didn't seem appropriate or necessary. That was fine with me. I simply wanted to spend my time enjoying this life and the benefits it provided. One of the main benefits that this life provided me was my new boyfriend. It all seemed so romantic! I began to feel safe around him and decided to share my recent past difficulties with him. There was an ease about our time together. There was much laughter and flirting. I would spend hours talking about politics, environmental issues, and campus life. I learned how to take control of my life. I learned about a higher power. I was able to create my own God based on my own understanding—sober, clear-minded, and intentional! That was my new purpose. I would conquer the world and make a difference. I was strong, smart, and able. Nothing could stand in my way. I would accomplish my dreams and create my future. I was in love and loved life. It all felt right and good.

Somewhere along the way, however, my personal dreams of telling people about Jesus through drama faded. I was spending more time with my boyfriend and less time focused on my theater classes. I did perform in the annual play, *Fiddler on the Roof.* It was amazing, and I had a blast. But as time went on, the reality of acting as a profession became less and less of a certainty. I doubted that my original plans would even fit into my new future. Drama and theater just didn't seem to be a realistic profession. I couldn't see how I could make a difference in the world with a career that had pretending as its foundation. It didn't seem to fit into the scheme of things. I tried to pray about it, but the God of my understanding didn't give me a clear answer. I was unable to make sense of it anymore. I began to doubt that it was something God had spoken to me in the first place. It even seemed that my old God had become silent on the subject. The thought of having my own career quickly vanished in the wake of my new love and my new God. Over time, my career was not even discussed. I embraced another path. The Bible tells us that we should be aware of the negative power that doubt can play in our lives. James 1:6–8 tells us that when asking God for wisdom, "Let him ask in faith, with no doubting, for the one who doubts is like a wave of the sea that is driven and tossed by the wind. For that person must not suppose that he will receive anything from the Lord; he is a double-minded man, unstable in all his ways" (ESV). Clearly, that verse described my soul's condition—doubting God and grabbing onto anything that made sense to me and felt good at that time—as unstable. My doubt and unbelief kept me from seeing the clear direction God had for me. I was making choices on my own, was accountable to no one, and tossed to and fro. I was focusing on my needs and not God's purpose. This ultimately directed and reinforced my life's trajectory. My need to be in control overshadowed all of my other choices. I would now have someone whom I could to love and who would love me. No longer would I be alone or lonely. This would be forever. Being the good girl, I knew that I would honor my vows: love, honor, cherish … forsaking all others …

We were married the very next year in that little yellow church. Family, friends, and our future all seemed wonderful. After a brief honeymoon, we moved back downstate to our familiar college town. I secured a job in the local hospital as a key punch operator. I lived paycheck to paycheck. Finances were limited, but I didn't care; I was in love and in control. In the evenings, I would entertain myself by watching TV or reading science fiction novels.

The following year, I found myself planning a trip to California to begin a new chapter in my life. I would truly be independent. I would be even farther away from our family, but I felt capable. I believed I could handle any challenge that would come my way. My new home would be located over three thousand miles away. I would be making my own decisions and setting my own course, accountable to no one, and my destiny would be of my own design. I was the master of my universe equipped with all I needed—my love for my husband and my future. I was off to change the world. The excitement was overwhelming.

I did not attend church at the time. I believed in the higher power I had created and behaved like I was invincible, able to do anything and everything I set my mind to. The fact that I didn't have a place to live in California didn't disrupt my plan, and neither did the concern that I didn't have a source of income deter me from moving forward. In fact, it seemed to add to the thrill of the adventure on which I was embarking. The uncertainty of it all intensified the level of excitement associated with such a bold move.

The trip across country was easy. I didn't veer off course or do any sightseeing. My goal was California or bust! Within the first week, just as I expected, I found housing and employment. I rented an apartment in Santa Rosa, California, and obtained a job in the Macy's key punch department store in San Francisco. The daily bus commute into the city was a bit of a hassle, but nothing was going to get in my way! I was sure I could handle it and overcome any obstacle that might come my way. I had my husband, fine friends, and a future plan: living life on my terms and living life to its fullest.

## My First Child

Then it happened—so unexpected. Maybe it was the stress of the commute. Maybe I was just mistaken. How could I be sure? Being so far away from family, I really couldn't just call Mom. That would have been a long-distance call, and I couldn't afford that. Medical issues were not in my plan. The symptoms indicated that there was something different. I wasn't sure exactly what it was. Or should I say, I wasn't sure I wanted to know what it was. I was only one week late, but I knew that was very unusual for me. In an effort to ease my mind, I asked one of my friends if she could give me reference for a doctor. I reassured her that I was sure it was nothing, but the curiosity was overwhelming, and not knowing wasn't an option.

Back in 1974, there weren't any over-the-counter medical testing strips for this. This type of medical testing was run in a laboratory. I made an appointment with her doctor. It seemed like the right thing to do. Just as she said, he was a gentle man and demonstrated confidence in his abilities. After a brief consultation, he agreed he should run some tests. Back then, it generally took a few days to a week for the results to come back from the lab. As mentioned earlier, patience was still not one of my strong points.

It was a Tuesday in late January when I was to hear from my doctor. I remember that day as clearly as if it had occurred yesterday. You see, the enemy used to replay this over and over in my head. He knew that it caused such grief in my heart and kept me bound. It would keep me shackled to grief, anger, betrayal, shame, and incredible self-loathing. There were years when I didn't have any defenses to combat the enemy's taunting and ridicule. When I would think back to these events, the mere thought of them felt like they would destroy me. My thinking, fears, and decision-making were all unbelievably distorted. The Bible helps us understand the truth of what is really going on in our lives when we go through experiences we just can't understand. I'm reminded of the story of Joseph. After many years of torment and trial, God reveals how all of Joseph's unkind, unexplained, and complicated experiences were needed to prepare him for God's mighty work. The wicked, unloving actions of his brothers were used by God to benefit and save many lives. It is recorded in Genesis 50:20, "You intended to harm me, but God intended it for good, to accomplish what is now being done, the saving of many lives" (NIV). God uses everything and everyone to accomplish His good work in our lives. We may not understand it at the time, but it is eventually revealed.

The week of waiting was very difficult. I found myself daydreaming about the possibilities. Could it be? I would have to quickly remind myself to not think along those lines. I had no clear, concrete evidence that such thinking was in order. Predictably, I made sure that nothing was discussed until I knew what I was dealing with. Like I said, it was a Tuesday in late January. As usual, I rode home from work on the bus that day. During the ride from San Francisco to Santa Rosa, nearly two hours, I kept thinking about the symptoms. Could it be? Should I get my hopes up? Should I let my guard down?

I kept thinking that maybe I was entering a new chapter in my life. The possibility that I might be having a baby was exciting and a bit scary. Although it wasn't part of my original plan, how wonderful it would be. I could make the necessary adjustment to my plan to make this work. Right? I was smart, clever, and the master of my future. How great it would be to bring in a new life. I could love and care for this child in special ways. What a thrill it would be for my mom and dad to come to California for the birth. Certainly, someone from work would give me a nice baby shower. I would have a colorfully decorated cake. It would have to be either yellow or green because I wouldn't know the sex until birth. There would be tiny booties and onesies. Either way, I knew it would be fine, I was invincible, right? Or perhaps, on the other hand, maybe I was just being reminded of the importance of not missing taking the pill. Either way, my life theme was in full swing. I would be able to figure this out."Don't worry, God. I've got this."

Well, my suspicions were confirmed: I was pregnant. I was so excited and couldn't wait to share the good news. I had surrounded myself with loving and kind people. All seemed to have had my best interest in mind. We spent time together, laughing and having a great time enjoying life. Certainly everyone would be happy about the news, right? Well, that wasn't going to be entirely the case. Much to my shock, when I shared this news, the responses were not all positive. Now, granted, there were some who were genuinely happy for me. But there were many others who spoke words of discouragement and warning. Unfortunately, those comments were the words that impacted me the most. Those were the statements that created fear and doubt deep within my heart. Those were the assertions that seemed to speak to reason, logic, and not just emotion. Those were opinions warning me of things like the financial difficulties and hardships associated with having a baby. Some even spoke about the possibility that this might negatively impact my marriage. The commentaries seemed so dire, so dark. I knew I was living paycheck to paycheck, but I didn't take time to really look at the effect this would have. They would ask questions like, "Where is the money going to come from when you have to quit work?" "How are you going to pay for the hospital bill?" "Do you have savings to cover your expenses while you are out of work?" "How are you going to feed the baby when you barely have enough money for food now?" "When you go back to work, how are you going to afford daycare?" "Where are you going to live? Your apartment complex doesn't allow children!" "You need to act now before it is too late. It isn't a baby yet. Abortion is your only logical option."

Wow, so unexpected, so unanticipated. Shouldn't this have been a joyous time? It became clear that instead of having wonderful news, I had a terrible problem. The conversations with these people went from bringing a life into this world to removing unwanted tissue. How was this happening? My heart broke every time someone would remind me of all the obstacles. I was really confused and scared. What should I do now? They made it clear that I had to make a decision quickly before it was too late. I had to fix it, but how? My mind raced to come up with an answer, a retort, a plan. I didn't want to fight with them. They loved and cared for me. I felt so alone. I'm sure some of them meant well, but it really didn't feel that way at the time. The thought of having a baby sounded wonderful to me even though I hadn't included this in my current life's plan or had much experience with children. I didn't even have any experience in babysitting other children in my younger years. But that didn't seem to matter. All I felt was a delight in the thought of having a child. Over the past few days, I had unknowingly developed a longing to love this child, to give this child a life of love and acceptance. Loving and caring for a sweet child would be a joy. Surely there would be diapers, late nights, and lost sleep. But the sound of the cooing of a baby, the sweet fragrance of their skin, the beauty in their eyes, and the chance to love and care for them would make up for all of that, right? But now people were saying that I had it all wrong. They were saying that it wasn't a baby yet. Was this all premature? Was I jumping the gun? Was I simply feeding a hidden longing in my heart to love and care for a child? Again, like I said, I was totally unprepared for this moment.

Admittedly, I was so wrapped up in the romance and excitement of having a child that the practical aspects of income, housing, and daycare never occurred to me until they brought them up. Once I got my head out of the clouds, the truth was all I had to go on was what my own limited understanding was able to reveal. All I could see was what was possible within my own abilities—or lack thereof. Clearly, having a baby now was not possible. At least, that was what everyone led me to believe. Even though my desire to live an adventurous life in California was the central theme of my move across country, the thought of financial hardship and homelessness was definitely not supposed to be included. I did not have the kind of strength or support for this challenge, much less the level of faith necessary to confront the long-term commitment required in raising a child. No, they must be right; this was far beyond my abilities. I simply couldn't see how I would be able to provide for this child.

Unfortunately, back then I didn't know anything about having a relationship with the all-loving God who provides for His children. We are told in the book of Philippians 4:14, "But my God shall supply all your need according to his riches in glory by Christ Jesus" (KJV). Again the Bible reminds us of God's faithfulness in times of trouble. In Deuteronomy 31:6, it states, "Be strong and courageous. Do not be afraid or terrified because of them, for the Lord your God goes with you; he will never leave you nor forsake you" (NIV).

The world wanted me to focus on my limited abilities, but in reality the God of this universe had a message to remind me that I was not alone, He was with me, and He would never leave me. Oh, how I love the truth of God's Word. However, not having the benefit of His powerful truth, I was left to tackle this problem in my own strength and inadequate understanding.

## My Private Battle

There were many conflicting emotions and thoughts. I found myself grasping for answers. *Come on, Neva, concentrate. Get control! You have to make sense of this! If I choose to have a baby now, how will I survive? I'm out here, 3,200 miles away from my parents. If I choose not to have a baby, how can I live with myself? Choose, Neva. You have to choose.* Those were the only words I could hear in my mind. Then like a beacon of reason, a moment of clarity, my panicking mind recalled, "Forsaking all others," my marriage vows. Wow! Where did that come from? Admittedly, as outlandish as this thought was, it did seem to give me a sense of relief. It would certainly justify giving up the chance to have a baby for a noble cause. If nothing else, it should eliminate one of the warnings about my marriage. I'm sure this would help ensure that at least that wouldn't be jeopardized. Just the fact that I was honoring a vow made me feel like it was the right thing. Never mind that this particular vow was never meant to be applied in this way. That really didn't even factor into my thinking. All I knew was that when I thought of the concept of forsaking others for the sake of my marriage, I had a renewed sense of being in control again. This was something I could clearly take charge of. I shouldn't let an unexpected turn of events overrule what I wanted for my life. To forsake, by definition, means "to abandon someone or something; to desert, discard." I certainly didn't want to abandon or desert my marriage, especially if it was for a bit of unwanted tissue. I could always have babies later on. The need to make a decision on my own was overwhelming. I was sure that would be acceptable. People would certainly understand that. The god of my understanding, the god I had created, would understand. Plus, women were doing this all the time now. It was even legal in California. Maybe those people were right. They kept professing that it was far too early for it to be a living person. They all said that it was too soon for it to be alive. *So maybe it is only a tissue and not a life after all,* I thought. I figured I would delay having a family. That would settle any unpleasantness and neatly fit into my original plan. It must be the right choice. I was probably making too much out of this and should just settle down. This way all would be back to normal; my life could just continue like nothing had happened. I wouldn't have to fight with anyone or be upset. And who knows? Maybe everyone would love me more for being so unselfish. I could go on with my life unscathed. I could control this. *I'm sure I can fix this,* I reasoned. And so, relying on my limited abilities, warped thinking, and swayed understandings, I once again embraced my method of dealing with uncertainty by taking control. "Don't worry, God. I've got this."

I find it amazing how deceitfully cunning the enemy can be. The thought of adoption was never in the discussion. The only options that were considered were to remove the tissue or suffer a life of poverty and uncertainty. The enemy is a master at twisting our thoughts around. I look back at my reasoning. I kept referring to the situation as if the life was not yet present, that it was a process not yet completed. It enabled me to embrace the implication that there wasn't a life at stake. Those phrases manipulated my thoughts, and in so doing, they were able to make the unthinkable something reasonable, convince me that the repulsive was attractive. Satan is truly the father of lies. Now, don't get me wrong, I take full responsibility for how I responded to the suggestions. However, without a strong moral foundation, a living relationship with the Savior, the truth of God's Word implanted in my heart, and an assembly of godly people for support, it became an easy task for the enemy to convince and persuade me to continue to focus on my selfish, self-centered life and perform the horrendous.

## The Confessed Choice

I began to openly review my options. There were absolutely no funds available to go back to Michigan. I had made it clear to my family that I could live in California on my own. Pride was a constant, demanding comrade, exacting more out of me every day. The thought of moving back home with a small baby would be admitting incompetence, and that wasn't going to be a realistic option. On the other hand, the task of raising a child this far away from my home in poverty didn't seem realistic either. Not to mention that the mere thought of it frightened me to death. How could I survive? I had no money, no job. The apartment complex I lived in didn't allow children. I would have to move and find new housing. Not an easy task when you are out of work with a small baby.

California was one of the few states that allowed legal abortions.

There were people who kept saying that if the pregnancy was terminated early enough, it was just the removal of tissue; life hadn't really begun. So maybe I should consider this medical procedure as a way of dealing with this dilemma after all. If they were right, then all my thoughts of a baby were premature. It wasn't a baby after all. However, admittedly there was a part of me, deep down in my heart, that didn't really think that was right. But the ramifications of listening to my heart were too painful. The thoughts of removing tissue instead of killing a baby were easier to live with. It would simply take care of things without guilt and shame. I wouldn't have to worry about losing my security or my future. Yes, I agreed that this must be the right answer. Besides, I was honoring my wedding vows that I had made before God. I was honoring my future by "forsaking all others." It seemed to me that I was able to check more boxes with the "abortion option" than with the "having a baby" option. It even seemed, in my distorted way of thinking, that the God of my understanding had made sure that I had moved to a state that permitted abortions. If I had stayed in Michigan, I wouldn't have been able to make this choice. I concluded, in light of all the evidence, that this was the right thing to do. My version of wisdom prevailed.

In the book of Proverbs, we are given verses to reveal true wisdom. There are countless verses that expose the truths about the human heart. Likewise, there are many verses that help us understand how deceptive and dangerous our thinking can be. In Proverbs 14:12, it states, "There is a way that appears to be right to a man, but in the end, it leads to death" (NIV). Oh, that I could have known the Scriptures back then! The Word of our Lord is so full of wisdom and truth. But I had set my course. I would choose to remove this tissue as soon as possible. I would make another appointment with the doctor and ask him what was involved in moving forward with the procedure.

Isn't it amazing how we can so easily to come up with words that don't seem so offensive? "Procedure." Proverbs 2:12 reads, "Wisdom will save you from the ways of wicked men, from men whose words are perverse" (NIV). It is remarkable how we can so easily select words to use that soften the repulsiveness of our actions. It's one of the many ways the enemy woos our hearts into believing his lies. It is one of his subtle and powerful tools of deception. He is a master of making the unthinkable thinkable; the unreasonable reasonable; the unholy holy. Whenever we choose man over God, we have taken a dangerous turn. In the book of Jeremiah, the Lord is instructing His people on the dangers of relying on man and man alone. He identifies the pitfalls of turning their hearts away from Him. "The heart is deceitful above all things and beyond cure. Who can understand it?" (Jeremiah 17:9 NIV).

One week later, I took a day off from work to have a consultation about the next steps. Somehow, I knew this was going to be more than just a routine doctor's visit. I would have to discuss the procedure. It almost seemed to me that I was living inside a movie. I felt like I was following a script written for someone else's life. It was all so surreal. As I drove to the doctor's office, doubt began to creep into my thoughts. I began to see that this was clearly not part of my original plan for my adventure in California. Inside my heart, it felt like I was taking a major wrong turn. I wondered whether the trajectory of my life was being altered. Would my life really ever be the same? The doubt of my decision began to grow in my heart. I began to question. Would this really be okay in God's eyes? Why did I feel such dread, such sadness? I found my heart racing. I would chastise myself, "Get hold of yourself, Neva. You have already gone over all your options." I had to pull myself together. I had to remember that I was able to do this. I was still in control even though it really didn't feel like it. *Be strong. "Don't worry, God. I've got this."*

When the doctor came into the room, he seemed genuinely happy. He wore a white lab coat with his name embroidered above the pocket: Dr. Jones, OB-GYN. He had read the test results. Congratulations were certainly in order. He extended his hand for me to shake. But much to the doctor's surprise, he received a handshake that was a bit cold and shaky. My handshake was not very cheerful. It set the tone for the visit. I explained that I couldn't afford to have a child right now. To have a child right now would endanger my precious plans. I had a future, and having a child now would jeopardize everything. Maybe it would make sense in a few years. Maybe I would be better equipped when better employment was secured and finances were more abundant. Maybe then I would be better suited to move in this direction of growing a family. But for now, I needed to focus on my plans, my desires, and my mission. I needed to remove the tissue before it was too late.

My physician listened intently. It seemed to me that he may have been well acquainted with this line of reasoning. I looked at the expression on his face, and it became clear that he had heard this justification before. Specifics may have been different, but the message was the same: I am in control of my body and my destiny. Nothing was going to get in the way of my own personal ambitions. My truths were founded on my personal beliefs, which were based on my desires and passions, limited to my own understandings and opinions. Creating life was in my hands alone. So not now, thank you; maybe later.

After a moment of reflection, he proceeded to shift gears and begin to reassure me that if I waited until I was able to afford children, I might never have any children. That comment was followed by an awkward silence and an uncomfortable chuckle. I sat steadfastly. My expression was emotionless and determined. I believe the doctor saw my desperate need to convince him of my decision. In reality, I was frantically trying to maintain my composure and reinforce my fragile convictions.

As the appointment continued, it became evident that the course of action was set. I simply needed to know about any of the possible risks involved. Then I could schedule the procedure. The doctor changed his approach and proceeded to reassure me that this was going to be nothing more than a routine medical procedure that I would experience, and then I could move on. No big deal. It struck me that I didn't remember seeing him in that light before. His lightheartedness was no longer obvious. His demeanor was straightforward, matter-of-fact, and clinical at best. I had to admit that surprisingly, I felt strangely reassured.

## The Procedure

It was a breezy, somewhat overcast day, a Friday. The weather was a bit chilly by California standards, but it was pleasant enough. I was to be at the hospital early in the morning to get registered and settled in. I was told I should be home by midafternoon. That was good news because I had planned on having dinner with some friends at their home later that evening, and I didn't want this to interfere. This was just a routine procedure after all, right?

Shortly after arriving, the nurse came into my ward. I didn't have a private or semiprivate room. There was simply a large room with multiple gurneys separated by white curtains. I was the first to arrive. When my nurse came in with her nurse's cap and white dress, she went over some paperwork. After a brief document review, all formalities and legalities were in order and signed. She reassured me that it was all part of the normal registration procedure and that I would be going down the hall in about a half hour. I could relax. I could smoke in the hospital back then, so I took out a cigarette and lit it. I was trying my best to be brave. The doctor said I wouldn't experience any pain other than what I may have had during my normal monthly cycle. Again, I was reassured that the procedure was standard, and I need not worry about anything. It seemed like an eternity before they came to get me. I was relieved that I was going to finally get this behind me once and for all.

While I was waiting, I noticed the other women coming into the ward. Some came alone, but most had someone with them—a boyfriend, mother, or close friend. I thought, *How could that be?* For years I saw abortions as a way for women to privately deal with their out-of-wedlock unpleasant situations. It helped women who needed to fix their sinful mistakes. "Sinful mistakes"—where did that come from? I was married. So why did this all of a sudden feel sinful? Was it the procedure that was sinful? Not pleasing the god of my understanding was one thing, but committing a sin? Well, that was something totally different. Funny, but up until this point, I had never seen my procedure as sinful. My heart was fading. I was losing grip on my logic and rationalizations. I began to frantically fight to discipline my thoughts. I had to get a grip, regain control of my resolve. This was no time to be emotional, no time to bring morality into the picture! This was nothing more than a medical procedure. Once again, I had to convince myself that what I was doing was right. I recited my vows: "Forsaking all others." *All I'm doing is discarding unwanted tissue.* I tried to fill my mind with images of women protesting for the right to choose, the right to have control of their own bodies. I fought to embrace thoughts that my choice was right and appropriate. But why did my heart start faltering with words like sinful? There couldn't be any sin here because I was just having tissues removed. Like I said, this was a medical procedure, not a moral decision, right?

In the midst of my desperate, panic-stricken conflict, a nice orderly strolled in. He reviewed the signed documents he had attached on his clipboard, verified who I was, and said it was time for me to go. And with that, off we went.

They gave me some medication to calm me down when we arrived in the hospital ward, but with all my mental contradictions and emotional free-for-alls, by the time I was ready to leave for the operating room, I was desperately struggling with dreadful and overwhelming thoughts that this decision was wrong and this was my sinful mistake. But there was no backing out now.

I knew then that I just wanted to block it out of my memory. By now it was feeling more wrong than right, and I didn't want to remember any of this, if possible. I quickly tried to remind myself that this was, after all, just a routine procedure. Oh, how wrong I was!

I don't remember the procedure because they administered anesthesia shortly after arriving in the operating room. Although they did medicate me and put me under, the entire experience was to live with me for years. Little did I know at that time that this was an experience that would impact the rest of my life. On every Mother's Day, at every Sanctity of Life event, and during abortion rally news reports, my heart and mind would return to this event. It would be this very moment, this single point in my life, that would haunt me and revisit me like a bad dream. I would never really be able to escape it. I would never be equipped to overcome the ramifications of this single decision on my own.

When the procedure was completed, I was wheeled into a hallway and waited for another orderly to take me back to the ward. There, back in the hospital ward, I was to wait for the medication to wear off and then check out, go home, and go on with life. No big deal.

That was when the most startling thing happened. I began to weep. Not just tear up—I began to uncontrollably sob. I don't believe I have ever experienced such a heart-wrenching moment in my life. Breathing became difficult and spasmodic. I couldn't control what sounded like the howling of an injured animal. The volume seemed to increase with each wail. A nurse came by and saw my pathetic condition. I could scarcely breathe, much less speak. My natural response was to apologize for such outbursts, but I couldn't help myself. She took my hand, patted it gently, and said, "Don't worry, honey. It is just the hormones adjusting. You will be fine in a little bit. Be sure to ask for something for your nerves before you leave, to help settle you down over the next few days. Most women experience what appears to be an emotional reaction. Let me reassure you, it is purely medical in nature. It will pass."

I'd be fine in a little bit? It would pass? Did she know what had just happened? It was at that moment that the reality of the lie became crystal clear. This was not the removal of a tissue—this was the death of my baby. On that breezy, somewhat overcast day, I had ended the life of my firstborn child. This was the end of my baby's life. This was the end of my life as well. My life was changed forever, never to be the same again. I knew that beginning that day, life going forward would have to follow a path of denial, distraction, deceit, and despair. How did I get here? What happened to that confident, self-reliant, purpose-driven, enthusiastic young woman?

In the book of James, we are given a clear explanation of how our lives evolve into such a state. He helps us better understand the process of sin. We all have experienced times when we just couldn't put our arms around how we got to such unholy places in our lives. No one is exempt. James 1:15 says, "Then, after desire has conceived, it gives birth to sin; and sin, when is full grown, gives birth to death" (NIV). When I look back at this and read this verse, I'm overcome and armed with the truth of what *really* happened. When we are equipped with the truth, we can always heal and move forward. So what did I learn? What was my desire that conceived sin? I thought I was a good girl, good wife, and good person. I had even deceived myself into believing that since I was honoring my wedding vows, that somehow this wasn't a bad or sinful choice. What desire could I have had that would have led to this? It didn't seem like a desire anymore at all. It felt more like despair.

Well, it was one of the oldest desires that always lead to the deepest despair. From the beginning of time, there was the deceiving lie that we could do things our own way, thinking I could do it my way, by myself, without needing anyone's help. "Don't worry, God. I've got this," was the mantra of my heart. Because of this misdirected focus, this ever-convincing lie, I lived a life filled with grief and a sense of betrayal for years and years. How could I have been so naïve? How could I have believed such propaganda? Had I come to the place of such selfishness, self-centeredness, that I couldn't decipher the lie from the truth? Well, the enemy made sure those questions, and many more, penetrated my mind and heart, constantly reminding me of my foolishness and condemning me for the murder of my firstborn.

How could I navigate through life knowing what I had done and who I had become? These thoughts haunted me for years. The guilt was overwhelming. I had to do something to shut it off. *Keep busy. Maybe that would work. Yes, that should work. Make sure I'm busy thinking of anything and everything else. Make sure my mind is always active. Don't allow it to go idle.* Because every time it did, the condemnation would set in. Maybe if I could focus on becoming a better me, then the haunting of my past would stop whispering in my ears. I began reading novels and self-help books on how to improve my self-esteem. Maybe there would be help in alcohol or pot. I was willing to do anything to keep away the torment. While some of these would provide temporary relief, it was, for sure, only temporary.

Much to my surprise, time seemed to be my most helpful friend. As the days and weeks went on, I began to think less and less about my firstborn child. The ability to live in a state of denial became easier and easier. The prospects of an unencumbered future seemed to expand, and life seemed to go back to normal—or so I thought. You know, that's the horrible thing about sin: unless it is dealt with, it festers and grows deeper into your soul. You may think it is gone, but in time you will have to face it.

## My Second Child—Redemption

Within two years, the thoughts surrounding this event no longer had a grip on me. Life was good, and the future seemed bright. It was then that I discovered I was pregnant once again. It didn't take long for the topic of how this pregnancy would affect my future came up. Once again the suggestion of having an abortion as a way to address my pregnancy and postpone a single-income scenario was entertained. I had experienced enough private guilt and shame that this time I was able to defiantly stand up and strongly reject any such a proposal. This time there was no choice to be made. No longer could I support, agree, or entertain the idea that what was growing inside me was anything but a life! This baby was going to come into this world and live a full, loving, and prosperous life if I had anything to do with it. And that was exactly what I said. Where did I get that courage, conviction, and strength? I believe the Holy Spirit must have intervened. Amazingly, the people who supported the abortion option backed down. They said that they were "just kidding." Well, I didn't find any humor in their suggestion at all. While feeling victorious, I still found myself struggling with the haunting thought, "What if I had stood up to them two years ago? Were they just kidding then?" I spent years beating myself up, thinking that if I could have been stronger; maybe I wouldn't have made that frightful decision. Oh, how the enemy will deceive and trap you if you are not prepared and on guard.

The economy wasn't doing well for the company I was working for at the time, and they decided to lay me off in my third month of pregnancy. I was going to have a baby, and that was that! I devised a plan to allow the unemployment benefits to pay for the hospital bills. Interestingly, the reduced finances didn't seem to be as big of a problem as initially expected.

On Tuesday, April 14, 1976, at 7:12 a.m., I gave birth to a healthy, beautiful daughter, who was six pounds one ounce and twenty-one inches long. She was the light of my life! Auburn hair, brown eyes, ten fingers, and ten toes—a masterpiece! She was such a good baby too. Labor was twenty-six hours, and she was worth every moment. How precious she was. I can't explain the joy and unsurpassed delight she brought into my life. I would sit for hours just watching her, hugging her, and kissing her. She was like a drug I couldn't get enough of. I would wonder what life had in store for her. I would constantly thank God for this beautiful blessing. People would even stop us at the park or at the store and admire how beautiful she was. I enjoyed her as I uncovered the treasures of being a mother. She was truly a gift from God. I was frequently overcome with the amazement that God would give me such a wonderful blessing in light of what I had done to my first child. Thank You, God!

Even though I was only living on one income, my unemployment was sufficient to keep her in diapers and us in meatloaf. But life is more than the money we make. It takes more than financial health. In order to live a full and glorious life, you need emotional health. Life involves how you treat the people you love, what you value, and where you use your gifts and talents. Most important, life involves giving your soul to God. Those were some of the things with which I began to struggle.

## My Breakdown

My daughter was two. I found that it began to become more and more difficult to interact with others. I had secured a job and placed her in daycare. By all outward appearances, life was good. As time went on, I found that my past began to creep into my present. It didn't present itself in any grand way. No, it started off in subtle ways. I began to doubt my abilities and question my self-worth. I was slowly shutting myself away at home, rarely venturing out. My life's existence consisted of getting up, dressing my daughter, going to work, picking her up from daycare, fixing dinner, bathing her, sending her to bed, and then retreating to bed myself. It felt like I was slowly dying inside. Even though all the outside activities looked normal—beautiful home, successful job, lovely daughter, and all the trappings of a beautiful, up-and-coming family—my life was a wreck. Slowly but surely, my past, secret sin was festering. It had never been removed from my heart and soul. It was growing into a cancer that was suffocating my ability to breathe in the joys of life. I began to have nightmares every night. I began dreaming that my daughter was trying to kill me. I couldn't escape the overwhelming fear and torment. The dreams became extremely violent and dreadful. I did everything I could to try to stay awake because if I fell asleep, they would assault me. Then they would wake me up in cold sweats. I found no relief. When I would fall back to sleep in exhaustion, they would simply return and pick up right where they had left off. It was horrible.

Finally, out of desperation, I called my oldest sister in Michigan. She suggested I see a psychologist. She felt that what I was exhibiting all the signs of a nervous breakdown. She suggested I have a neighbor watch the baby and added that maybe I should take a walk to try to gather my thoughts. In the meantime, she would contact a psychologist, secure plane tickets for my baby and me, and check with her husband to see if we could live with them during my treatment. It was pretty radical, but it all seemed like a good plan.

I wasn't a member at any specific church, although I did make a point of having our daughter baptized when she was three months old. I didn't have a church family to go to or confide in, but I'm not sure I would have sought anyone out for guidance anyway. The guilt and shame that I felt were overwhelming. It certainly wasn't something I wanted others to know about. I definitely didn't think anyone would want to be my friend if they knew what I had done. Per my sister's instructions, I loaded up the baby and took her to my next-door neighbor's home. My neighbor was an older woman in her midfifties. She loved my daughter and enjoyed watching her from time to time, so there was nothing unusual about my request. She didn't say anything about my appearance, though—red face, tear-stained eyes, and disheveled hair. I think she understood more than I gave her credit for at the time. My walk wasn't brisk; I really took my time. I needed to try to be quiet and sort things out. Everything seemed to be unraveling. Everything seemed to be slipping away. I had to get my control back. I knew I had messed up my life so badly that even my mantra was no longer working. It wasn't even a part of my thoughts. I truly didn't have this.

There was a small church nearby. The thought to go inside

and pray became strong. I ventured in. Surprisingly, the doors were unlocked. I entered into that quiet, peaceful sanctuary. I almost felt like I was back in Hermansville, Michigan, in my old yellow church. I walked slowly, taking in the atmosphere. It was quiet and peaceful. There was that special church smell. I guess it comes from the polish on the pews. It seemed soothing nonetheless. I moved into one of those pews and began to pray. I really don't remember much of what I prayed about. Certainly, there were prayers asking for direction, prayers asking for the pain and fear to stop. But most of all, I just remember needing to be in quiet in this peaceful place.

At the time, all seemed lost and dark, but God was weaving His healing. I didn't know that at the time, but He was laying the foundation for me to see His healing in my life instead of the pain, His plan instead of my plan. He was going to use my darkness as a backdrop to shine His everlasting light. We can't have a victory without a battle, and mine had just begun.

Time passed, and I found myself slipping back from a place of peace and rest into my troublesome reality. I was not sure how long I had been resting in there, but the sun was beginning to set, and I needed to get home and face the possibility of my leaving to get some much-needed mental and emotional help.

The decision was made; arrangements were in order. Two plane tickets were waiting for me at the San Francisco Airport. My sister had made an appointment with the psychologist, and a warm bed was waiting for us at her home. The thought of me leaving for an unknown amount of time with our daughter seemed to be a rational plan. I spent the rest of the evening packing for my daughter's and my trip. Later that night, we drove to the San Francisco Airport. Still somewhat dazed by the events of the day, my daughter and I caught the red eye to Detroit to begin a time of what was hoped would be a season of rest and healing.

My sister met us at the airport. She had arranged for me to meet with the psychologist that afternoon. We drove to her home and quickly unpacked. My brother-in-law agreed to watch my daughter.

Things seemed to be moving quickly. It was a Saturday. I was a bit surprised that the therapist would see us on the weekend, but my sister was very concerned and had convinced him I needed to be evaluated as soon as possible.

He seemed nice enough. He was soft-spoken and walked with a limp. He asked me a lot of questions about the topic of harm. He wanted to know if I felt like I was going to harm myself or anyone else. I said no. The thought of harming anyone else had never entered my mind. Quite frankly, I had done enough of that years ago. But the thought of harming me, well, that was totally different. Thoughts of harming me were constant. I would contemplate ways to end the pain daily. The thoughts of killing me were killing me. I didn't want to live like this, in such torment and despair. Quite frankly, if it hadn't been for my precious daughter, I might have already harmed myself. As we continued to explore my current condition, I realized that this man made me feel safe. I felt at ease with him and was able to open up. Upon the conclusion of our session, he determined that although these thoughts were concerning, I wasn't a real danger to myself or anyone else. I didn't need to be on any medication. He felt he could help me more efficiently if I was not drugged and in as clear a mind as possible.

I met with him for six weeks, seven sessions a week. I had no idea how intensive this schedule would be, and neither did I anticipate how demanding each session would be. Every session was very emotional and required hours of daily journaling. We discussed many topics. We started with a brief history. My drinking patterns in college and the date rape were the first areas we considered. We discovered I was not an alcoholic after all. We were able to uncover the wounds associated with my date rape, and I was able to obtain long-needed healing. It was all very intensive. Nothing seemed to be out of bounds in terms of exposing the pains and heartaches in my life. I was beginning to experience healing.

During one of my sessions, we discussed my hidden secret, my abortion. I began to talk about it openly. In the beginning, much of our conversation was focused on how betrayed I felt by my friends. Isn't it interesting how easy it is for us to find fault and blame others for the decisions for which we are ultimately responsible?

Slowly, the realization that I had played the key role in the decision gave way to a deeper understanding of why I had come to see myself in such a wretched manner. I could no longer ignore that my heart could be as dark as coal even though on the outside looked bright and clean. Oh, what deception hides in our hearts!

My counselor encouraged me to see the power of positive thinking. He continually reminded me that all I had to do was change the way I was thinking. It was time for me to redirect my thoughts. I needed to think about how I loved my daughter, and that was all that mattered. It was a clear indication that I truly loved children. The past was over. There was no bringing my baby back. I needed to move on. He wanted me to spend more time focusing on the circumstance of the event. He felt that the cards had been stacked against me. We discussed the overwhelming negative comments that had ultimately influenced my decision. Clearly, I had been at an unfair disadvantage. He insisted that this was the way I needed to frame the decision I had made. By doing so, it would help me realize that I was innocent of any deliberate wrongdoing. The key word here was *deliberate*. He told me that I was a product of my circumstance, that I was just as much a victim as my baby. I needed to open my mind and accept new realities.

He used a popular treatment that was centered on understanding a person's behavior and her relationships. It focused on the idea that our reactions to the experiences of life were the direct result of our understanding of life. It was our individual discernment that molded our personalities and our approaches to life in general. With enough information, we were able to control our lives. This made sense to me. It verified my long-owned viewpoint that all I had to do was stay in control. I needed to learn how to reframe my circumstances in my mind. I needed to stop blaming me for things that were out of my control. I needed to regain control and all would be better. Wow.

In essence, all I had to do was embrace the concept that there were things and people in life I couldn't control—they were not my fault, and so I should buck up and think rationally. Then I could better control my emotions and make better decisions. I was accountable to no one. I was a master unto myself. I had to take back my life! It was entirely based on what I was willing and able to do. It seemed like we were simply redefining my life's mantra: "Don't worry, God. I've got this." As long as I was able to do it and make sense of it, it would get better. It was entirely based on my strength, my insight, and my abilities. As we continued to discuss many issues, I found it easier and easier to remove myself from any wrongdoing and take charge of my future choices. I began to realize that I was in this shape because of circumstances that I had let get out of my control. I had become mentally and emotionally lazy. Everything seemed to suggest that all I had to do was work harder at my self-image and adopt a new way of thinking, and that would solve most of my problems. The nightmares had stopped, so I thought I must be on the right track.

## My Reconciliation

After six weeks of therapy, I had made some major strides in my ability to cope with life. I had renewed some old tools and obtained some new ones that would assist me along life's journey. But would that be enough to stand the test of time? We spent many hours discussing how I had changed and how things would need to continue to change. We discussed whether or not I was willing to do what appeared necessary to have a successful life going forward. No doubt about it, I felt energized and invigorated. I was committed to having a positive life and future. I was capable of making new decisions and having new outlooks. With a deep breath and a clearer resolve, I decided to try again with this fresh approach and perspective. Armed with a sharper focus and scheme on how to best deal with life, we flew back to California to begin a new chapter in my life.

I felt better for a time. But my new way of approaching life still only addressed what I could control and understand. Clearly, this was going to be a limited venture. Nothing would really give me lasting peace.

Now, this process of positive thinking may have been a great method of treatment for a temporary fix. But it never addressed the real issue: sin. How could it? It didn't deal with the looming reality that when I had taken my life into my own hands and behaved according to my standards to suit my own needs, it was then that my life had begun to fall apart. My limited abilities were just that—limited.

I didn't know it at the time, but I had it all backward. There was no way I could, in my limited self, overcome such a transgression. What could I ever do to fix this deed of death? It would have to require a supernatural, sacrificial intervention. I now know that it is only when I surrendered my life and accepted Jesus's sacrifice on the cross for my sin that I could experience true freedom. I didn't need to just understand the sin; I needed the sin to be completely removed. And that was something I could never do. Instead of filling my mind with limited thinking, I had to fill my heart with the boundless love of Christ. I had to empty myself to be filled up with a fresh, clean life. But to surrender would mean I would have to admit my life was out of my control again, and I wasn't willing to go there. That was against all I had learned and believed in. That would mean I would have to trust Jesus. I thought I had already tried that. My experience in Hermansville seemed short-lived. Then there was the time when I had tried to approach Jesus in college. I remembered how it had seemed like Jesus didn't like me. How could I let Him take control of my life? I remembered the scorn and disgust I had felt from others. I didn't think I could handle Jesus's condemnation and ridicule for all I had done now. Drinking, partying, and not attending class were one thing, but this? Well, it was beyond my ability to comprehend how a holy God could love such an unholy person. No, exposing me to Jesus was not going to be my answer.

I didn't understand that to trust Him would give me the true freedom I was seeking. In Romans 8, Paul talks about the believer being freed from the condemnation of sin. To be freed from the guilt and shame of my sin was what I was truly seeking. Not another method, program, or activity. That would not do. I needed a total makeover, a total takeover, a real life change. The Bible teaches that when we accept what Christ did for us on the cross and follow Him, we are then free from the law of sin and death. That is because the law—our performance, our abilities alone—is powerless to give us the peace and freedom our hearts so desperately seek. The apostle Paul talks about moving from a life that is controlled by our sin nature and embracing the life controlled by God and the Holy Spirit. Not living by the flesh but living by the Spirit. The law of performance is limited to only my abilities. The freedom of the Spirit is boundless.

The true freedom we seek comes only through Jesus's sin offering on the cross. It is then that we can experience the transformed minds spoken of in Romans 12. In verse 2, the Bible tells us, "Do not conform to the pattern of this world, but be transformed by the renewing of your mind" (NIV). This isn't referring to a mind that we renew but a mind that the Holy Spirit renews. The transformed mind He refers to occurs when we allow the Holy Spirit to speak to us and control our thoughts and our actions. A mind that will truly empower us comes when we reject the world's requirements of self-reliance and autonomy and embrace the truth of God's Word. It is about what Jesus did at the cross, not what I do. It is when we listen to His voice, the prompting of the Holy Spirit, that we can then understand, study, and embrace God's Word. His Word and His Word alone has the elements necessary to accomplish the needed transformation for true healing and release from the bondage with which sin shackles us. Until we look at ourselves and see our lives from God's point of view, the Creator's perspective, we will never truly experience freedom from the bondage of sin. And don't be mistaken—it is true bondage. We may be able to whitewash it with some clever opinions, philosophies, or programs for a time, but none of that is eternal.

## My Third Child—Joy Unspeakable

Within three months of returning home, I discovered I was going to have another baby. This time the suggestion regarding abortion was not even discussed. On Friday, September 5, 1980, at 6:47 p.m., we gave birth to an amazingly wonderful baby boy: seven pounds fifteen ounces, twenty-two inches, peach fuzz hair, brown eyes, ten fingers, and ten toes. I couldn't have been more delighted. I had never understood the special bond that God has for a mother and her son. But when my son was born, I was overwhelmed with a love I had never experienced before. He gave me much joy. When I held him, he seemed to look deep into my heart. There was an amazing connection between us. He truly had my heart.

My days with my daughter and baby son were delightful. We seemed to be a real family now. *Maybe I will be okay after all,* I thought. I just needed to focus on facts. I had been blessed with two beautiful, healthy children; finances were fine; and health was good. All I needed to do was focus, keep my thoughts positive, not dwell on the past, and maintain a positive outlook. I needed to continue to be intentionally self-reliant. Certainly, that would guarantee that all the ugliness of my past would be behind me. I could move into a bright and prosperous future. That performance-based, controlled thinking worked for a few years. But it wasn't to last—no surprise there.

Ever so slowly, attitudes and sentiments began to erode. There grew a steady undercurrent of dissatisfaction. There was an unsettling atmosphere in our home. It seemed like I had to navigate through it daily. Disagreements on a variety of issues and life in general became the norm. I had begun attending church. It wasn't long before I disagreed on the way our church worshiped. I was dissatisfied with just about everything when it came to church. Even sermon messages seemed to fuel my deepening discontent. My discussions with others were passionate, to say the least. Interestingly, though, they never seemed to mean anything or resolve anything. They seemed to be a way to vent my growing annoyance with everyone. I struggled in an effort to keep positive and strong. I had to maintain a high level of self-worth. I couldn't go back to that dark time again.

My most popular method of interaction was usually demonstrated by ignoring people. I began to distance myself from others again. I limited my conversations. I avoided addressing my real issues with anyone because to walk down the path of truth was too dangerous, too painful. Truth be told, I was absolutely not equipped to survive that journey. I did not possess the sufficient knowledge, emotional strength, or communicational tools required to conquer those demons. I simply had to continue acting as if everything was fine. I became an expert at subtle lies and deceptions. There was an escalating sense of distrust. I began to feel unloved and unappreciated. I started to think that I was never going to be happy. Nothing seemed to satisfy—not home, not employment, not friendships, not even the occasional church activities. And of course, there was always that secret sin to haunt me. Freedom from the guilt and shame became impossible. The only joy I really had was with my children. Those precious souls were innocent. With them, I could love and be loved unconditionally. Their lives were genuine, open, and untarnished. They were not a constant reminder of my sin. Unfortunately, my private thoughts were. They constantly reminded me of my painful past and gave me no hope of a promising future.

## The Wilderness Years

It wasn't long before I sought comfort outside our home. I was working in a well-known manufacturing company. I enjoyed my work and the people in my department. There were people from all walks of life there: young and old, foreign-born and native-born, handicapped and athletic, gay and straight—people whom I would have never met if I had stayed on the farm. Among this group of hardworking people was a young man who seemed interesting. He seemed to have a gentle spirit, was easy to talk to, and seemed genuinely interested in my plight. We began sharing our life's journeys, and there grew chemistry between us. This type of relationship was totally normal and acceptable in this liberal, free-living, openly loving environment in California. As time went on, it became apparent that I was no longer content at home. After fourteen years of marriage, I decided to file for divorce. The legal term I filed under was "non-contested irreconcilable differences." Amazing, isn't it? The thought of my marriage vows didn't seem to play into that decision—in sickness and in health, for better or worse, for richer or poorer, till death do us part. There was nothing about honoring or cherishing. Again, my sinful, selfish desire was dictating my sinful actions and decisions. The desire to be in control of my life was still my paramount motivation. Because I could not figure out a way on my own to be happy in my marriage, I relied on the answer that *was* in my control: find someone else who could make me happy and get a divorce. "Don't worry, God. I've got this!" I ended up without him after all. So much for "forsaking all others." The enemy knew exactly where my weak points were. He convinced me that all I had to do was rely on my abilities, my knowledge, my opinion, and my strength. In doing so, I not only lost my baby and my marriage, but most of all, I had clearly lost my way. At the time, I didn't see it that way, but it is not surprising that I felt duped nonetheless.

I lived with this man for the following year. It felt like I had finally found my true love. But that was not the plan God had for me. I became obsessed with my children's welfare, and he was no longer my primary interest. Not surprisingly, the relationship didn't last more than one year. Once again I was alone, having to navigate life by myself. I spent the year wandering in and out of relationships, in and out of bars, in and out of life. Some relationships actually felt fulfilling, but none of them filled the hole that was left in my heart. It seemed like the more I tried to fix my life, the worse it got. The hole in my heart began to feel like a sinkhole subtly growing deeper and wider.

## My Seeking Year

In desperation, I decided to try going back to church. This time, there was an overwhelming desire for answers. I wasn't going because my parents were going or because it was the right thing to do. My seeking was extremely personal, not a social interaction. The tables had turned. I was now at a place of surrender. It had become very clear that my way wasn't working.

I remembered how wonderful I had felt in my small church in Hermansville, Michigan. I remembered the peace I had experienced in that church during my walk the day before I went into therapy. Maybe I could regain some of that peace. Maybe that would be the answer—a personal moment with God.

There was eagerness in my seeking this time. There *had* to be something bigger, stronger, and more powerful in life. The higher power I had created didn't seem to have the answers or even the power to help me. Maybe it was time for me to reexamine Jesus. I was even willing to engage with the Jesus whom my roommate had told me about. I clearly knew that I had messed up my life—abortion, adultery, divorce, immoral living. I was sure He wasn't happy with me now. But maybe He would be able to understand what I was going through. Maybe He could extend some of that mercy I had heard about in Sunday school. I remembered the felt board lessons when Jesus had helped people who were lost and sinful. There was the story about the woman at the well, and what about that account where the men were going to stone the adulterous woman? Clearly I could relate to the condition of those women. I obviously fit that bill. Didn't Jesus help them? Those women seemed to be out of options too. They needed someone to help them for sure. It was apparent that I was no longer the master of my destiny. Or should I say that the destiny I was the master over was crumbling. I had to find someone with the answers on how to fix the mess I'd made of my life! Maybe Jesus was the answer.

It was during this time that I felt the overwhelming need to purchase a Bible. I decided that if I was going to investigate Jesus, I should have the one book that was considered the main source on the topic. I wanted to make sure I found a Bible that made sense to me. I remembered when my pastor would read the Bible from the pulpit. There were a lot of words that seemed strange. King's English was what they called it. That version was confusing to me. I found myself spending more time trying to understand the words than understanding the message. I wanted a Bible that I could understand and that would help me understand this God who seemed to be calling me back home. There weren't many Christian bookstores in my town, but I was able to locate one in the strip shopping mall near my apartment. I must have spent hours reading and reviewing the different versions and translations, print sizes, study Bibles, and devotional Bibles. There seemed to be an endless amount of options from which to pick. Finally, I found one that was written in a way that I could understand. It had a great study feature that helped guide me to a deeper understanding. I really can't explain it, but when I picked it up, it felt right. I spent many evenings sitting at my dining room table, reading and trying to understand what He wanted me to do and be. When I opened it up to read it, it felt like I was sitting down with a dear friend. This Jesus seemed kinder than the one I remembered in college. His words seem to speak to me like no other. There was a sense that He knew me more than I thought, like He was revealing truths about me that I didn't even know existed. There was newness, freshness, and brilliance when I read my Bible.

I remember one day in February 1988. While making my bed,

of all things, the thought came to me that I needed to believe what I was reading in the Bible. It was a revelation for sure. I was not going to pick and choose which verses I would follow. Everything would be important and true for me. Either it was all true, or none of it was true. It was at that moment that I really began to feel the power of the Scriptures. I experienced a hunger for all of it. A true gift from God Himself!

I began looking for a church on my own and seeking God like never before. There was an excitement in my heart. Was I beginning to meet the Jesus whom my roommate had spoken about?

The church I found initially wasn't a strong, Bible-teaching church, but it was a denomination I had been affiliated with in the past. They had some great fellowship, and that helped me feel like I wasn't alone. But the lack of Bible study support became an issue. I didn't want to fall into the trap of focusing on the fellowship at the expense of obtaining a deeper understanding of what I was reading in my new Bible. That hadn't worked in the past, and I was sure it wouldn't work now.

I shared this amazing revelation about believing the whole Bible with my friends at the church I was attending. To my shock, they didn't agree. They said that the Bible was a great book but that it was more of a reference guide than an authoritative manuscript. Wow. Even though I didn't have a degree in theology, I knew that wasn't right. I knew that the truths that I was uncovering in my reading time were real, specific, and absolute.

It wasn't long before I found myself studying the Bible by myself again. My church attendance began to dwindle until I no longer attended. But my Bible reading was amazing!

How long had it been since I had found such peace and comfort? Ten, twelve years. It felt like an eternity since I had experienced this kind of peace and reassurance in life and in my future. As time went on, my hunger for the Word became stronger and stronger. It seemed like the more I read, the more I wanted to read.

It was during these moments of reading the Bible that the Lord revealed Himself to me. It was like my heart ached to hear His voice. The truth is God wants us to know Him intimately. He wants us to have a personal encounter, a personal relationship with Him. He is passionate in speaking directly into our hearts. His Word says, "You will seek me and find me when you seek me with all your heart" (Jeremiah 29:13 NIV). When I read that verse, I knew that was exactly what I was doing, seeking Him with my whole heart, and He was speaking to my whole heart.

His Word also says, "Taste and see that the LORD is good" (Psalm 34:8 NIV). What did that mean? How could I taste God? Much of my understanding about God was from my childhood. The age-old stories that were read to me in Sunday school were the foundational understanding that I had of God. He was the Creator in the Genesis story, He was the Deliverer in Exodus, and He was the Savior in John. All of that knowledge was great, but I really had never experienced Him. The experience in Hermansville, Michigan, had been wonderful but not life-changing. I experienced Him that night, but I didn't allow Him to enter my heart. It was like when I left the church that night, I left Him there too. I didn't ask Him to walk with me. I simply left Him. Watching a movie and living a life are two separate encounters. One is short-lived; the other lasts a lifetime.

To know Him, to taste Him, was something beyond my understanding. How do you really get to know God in such a way that you can taste Him? Little did I know that the Creator of the universe had a personal plan for my life. That plan was to know Him intimately. I had to surrender my will. I had to accept, adopt, and embrace His will. You see, when I decided to live life on my terms, I received only that which was in my limited abilities. I was bound by the limited capabilities of those around me. But when I decided to live life on God's terms, I was given all of His infinite abilities and possibilities. My life was about to be radically changed.

# *My Salvation*

Friday, September 29, 1988, was my thirty-fifth birthday. The young man whom I had lived with after leaving my husband invited me to a small, out-of-the-way church drama event. They were hosting a drama group from the East Coast. During the previous year, he too had been searching for answers. Earlier that summer, he had stumbled upon a small evangelical church and had been saved. He called me and told me. He was so excited! He almost sounded like my college roommate. I acted like I knew what he was talking about, but I truly didn't. I think he knew it because my responses to his good news were sterile and formal. "Oh, I'm so happy for you. Isn't that nice." These comments were clearly not the kind of response one would expect from someone who has experienced the saving grace of Jesus Christ. He wanted me to have a saving relationship with Christ, and so he waited for the right time to introduce me to the Jesus he had come to know and love. Isn't it amazing how God uses not only our poor life decisions but also the people involved in them to bring us home? His detailed orchestration of our lives and those around us is beyond my comprehension.

My friend knew it was my birthday and that I enjoyed theater. He also knew that I was desperately seeking God on my own. He believed that this could be an event that I would enjoy and hopefully hear the salvation message of the Gospel. Little did I know that he had been praying for weeks that God would show up and invite me to receive His forgiveness for my sins.

I was excited to see him again. I had to admit I still had feelings for him, but it was clear that this relationship would never be anything more than special friends. At the end of the presentation, the visiting pastor gave what I later learned was an altar call. I had never witnessed anything like that before. People were getting out of their seats and walking up to the front of the sanctuary. Many were weeping. All were kneeling with their heads bowed in prayer. Clearly, they were all having a personal moment with God.

The pastor kept repeating the Scripture verse from the book of Matthew: "Whosoever therefore shall confess me before men, him will I confess also before my Father which is in heaven. But whosoever shall deny me before men, him will I also deny before my Father which is in heaven" (Matthew 10:32–33 KJV).

Ever so slowly, the Holy Spirit began to work on my heart. Every time the pastor repeated the verse, the verse seemed to speak to me clearer and clearer. Had I been living a life denying Christ? Had I been holding myself up in higher regard than Jesus? Was I being denied before the Father? Something broke inside of me at the thought that the loving Jesus I was learning about in my Bible would deny me before His Father. It was then that I understood that I had never confessed Jesus! It was the *relationship* with Christ that made the difference, not the religion. I realized that I could tell you all about the stories in the Bible, but until now, none of them had me in them. My experience of God was all outside of me but never inside me. I had never taken the time to make Christ the center of my life before. Never had I made a commitment to follow Him either privately or publicly. This pastor was telling me that I needed to make that public confession—a confession that I was going to follow Christ from this day forward. I needed to trust Christ with my heart and my sin, to let Him right my wrongs. I had to make a declaration that I was going to accept the forgiveness that He offered me because of what Christ did, not what I did. I had lived my life backward! The whole purpose of Jesus's life was to forgive me of my sins. He had to die so that I could live. Finally, I had found my required supernatural, sacrificial intervention.

Christ shed His own blood on the cross. Without the shedding of blood, there could be no forgiveness of sin. No one else had the blood needed to accomplish such a remarkable feat! Because He was God, He had the DNA in His blood to cure the disease of sin. He had paid the price for my sin, and He wanted me to accept that forgiveness.

I was overwhelmed with excitement. I finally understood what was needed to become whole again, and it overpowered me. The amazing truth was that the Creator, God, wanted me to be in His life. He wanted to heal me, love me, comfort me, guide me, and give me a fresh start!

The visiting pastor quoted Romans 5:8; "While we were still sinners, Christ died for us" (NIV). I recognized at that very moment that Christ loved me with a love I had never known. He knew about everything in my life. He knew my thoughts, my motives, and my heart, and He still died for me so that I could be forgiven and live with Him forever. How could that be? What unbelievable love! Finally, the answer, the solution, the remedy was right there before me: Jesus Christ, the Son of God. Only He could heal my sin-sick soul. I had spent so many years trying to find my own way and continually trying to figure everything out using my own understanding of things, eventually leading me to a place of utter confusion concerning life, love, purpose, and direction. The Bible talks about how Jesus has the answers to all of this. There is the passage when Thomas, the disciple of Jesus, wanted to know where Jesus was going and how they would know the way. It is right after Thomas confesses Jesus to be his Lord that he asks Jesus about how to know the way. In John 14:5–7, it says, "Thomas said to him, 'Lord, we don't know where you are going, so how can we know the way?' Jesus answered, 'I am the way and the truth and the life. No one comes to the Father except through me. If you really knew me, you would know my Father as well. From now on, you do know him and have seen him'" (NIV). I remembered my college roommate. This must be her Jesus, the one about whom she was always beaming. No wonder she couldn't stop talking about Him.

## *My New Life in Christ*

And so there it was. Jesus was the way. He was all that was needed. I didn't need to perform, keep up appearances, or figure anything out. I simply had to accept Jesus, confess Him as my Lord, and follow Him.

That evening, I understood the true meaning of love. I found myself running to the altar to meet this personal Jesus. I told Him how sorry I was for living a life of rebellion, self-reliance, and disobedience. I wanted Him to rule my life. He was going to take control. I wanted to give up my way of doing things and follow Him. How could I have missed this? He is the Master of the universe and the Creator of my life. No wonder He has all the answers. He knows all the avenues to true peace.

I prayed that this wasn't going to be just another twelve-step program, another psychological theory, another mental exercise. I prayed that this would be forever. I prayed that He would never leave me. I begged that this would finally be something of substance, something that I could hold onto for the rest of my life. I prayed that this wasn't a temporary fix. Immediately I felt a peace and a reassurance that I had found what was missing in my life. What blessed assurance!

He saved my soul on my thirty-fifth birthday. I was so overcome by the presence of God in that little church in northern California. There, I met the Lover of my soul, the One who knew all about me, my cover-ups, my hang-ups, and my give-ups. He knew about my fears and my confusion. But most of all, He knew about my secret sin, and amazingly He loved me unconditionally anyway. He created me and loved me with an everlasting love that exceeded all rational thinking. How could I have missed this years ago? The Master of the universe loved me so much, and He wanted to spend eternity with me so desperately that He sent His only begotten son to die for my sins. "For God so loved the world, that he gave his only begotten Son, that whosoever believeth in him should not perish, but have everlasting life" (John 3:16 KJV). I had heard that all my life but never understood what it truly meant and how it would apply to my life—until that night.

It was crystal clear. He knew what I needed. He gave up His

child to die a horrible death, even death on a cross, so I could be free and alive with Him. His decision was a sacrificial, loving gift. It was selfless, sacrificial, and completely full of love for me. My life was changed forever, and I was given a fresh start. The freedom from sin's guilt and shame didn't come as the result of my limited abilities or my ability to keep positive. Instead, it came from the unlimited, unmerited grace from the heavenly Creator, Father God. He had this plan for me from the beginning of time. He knew all the decisions I was going to make, all the wrong turns I was going to take. He had already established a rescuer for me—His Son, Jesus Christ. What exhilarating freedom! What amazing grace! What divine love!

That was the beginning of my life. Truly, it was the beginning of a journey that continues today. Much has happened since that wonderful day. I have grown to know Him more and more every day. Reading the love letters that He has written for me in His Bible has helped me have a better understanding of what this life is all about. I have laughed and cried. I have been challenged and have basked in the rest of His arms. He has time and time again rescued me from myself. To receive the unmerited love and grace from the holy Creator is an awesome gift that I treasure daily. There have been times when I didn't understand what His will was for me, but He has always been faithful to reveal it at the perfect moment, not too soon and never late.

So there you have it: a life that was designed by God, loved by God, and created for God. It was wonderfully made—all of It! It consisted of some normal, everyday events alongside some events that were a bit more tragic and life-changing. But in the middle of all of it, His mighty, loving, and redemptive hand was moving me ever so closely to His heart. He hasn't wasted a thing. He uses all my joys, heartaches, sins, and victories for His glory. He orchestrated my life to become a testimony of His greatness, His far-reaching mercy, His unconditional love, and His undying forgiveness. Only by revealing His glory in the mist of my weakness could He manifest His majesty so clearly that others could see! Amazing—He wastes nothing. All of our lives are for His glory. Daily, He shows me new mercies and gives me insights into His eternal love and passion. When I thought I was at my lowest, He profoundly blessed me with the very life I thought I had destroyed. I still find it remarkable that the God of this universe would have such an intimate and specific plan for me. I hold onto the verse in Psalm 119:130, "The unfolding of your words gives light; it gives understanding to the simple" (NIV).

Needless to say, I now have a totally different motivation for my life. No longer do I feel it necessary to operate in my own strength or knowledge. My new mantra now comes from my heavenly family. They gently and lovingly whisper in my ear, "Don't worry, Neva. We've got this!"

The rules I learned when I was younger still apply. But now they have a deeper meaning in my life. They speak to why these basic childhood rules are so powerful.

- Stay within our neighborhood
  - Follow the Word of God
- Be home before the streetlights came on
  - Stay in the light of My love; flee from darkness
- Share with others
  - Go out into the world and share the Gospel
- Always be kind to one another
  - Love your neighbor as I have loved you

Now that God is in control of my life, He has given me an overwhelming, powerful desire to share this amazing relationship with others. I see people struggling with the circumstances and situations in their lives. We need to remember that we need not worry about the circumstance or situation that He brings into our lives. It is what He brings out of our lives that have real significance. He uses our free will for His glory, even when we are in rebellion.

I don't ever want to forget that the loving Father has a perfect plan for our lives. Even when all seems lost, when we go our own way and experience brokenness, He still has an established plan for His glory. He wastes nothing and no one. All creation is for His glory.

Without a doubt, God has miraculously taken my brokenness for the purpose of healing.

He has taken my damaged past and given me a divine purpose.

My journey, my life had just begun!

# Unfinished Business: Let the Deep Healing Begin

I had been walking with the Lord for about ten years. I eagerly attended church and was open about sharing my faith with others. I was active in my church choir, Missions Ministry, and drama group. Other than this issue concerning my past secret sin, my life was relatively peaceful and fulfilling. On the outside, there was absolutely no evidence of my concealed battle. Believe me, no one would have ever suspected my past. In fact, for many this book will be a revelation.

However, as time went on, I found myself more and more preoccupied with memories of my abortion. I didn't experience anything radical at first, just brief moments of recollection—reflection, if you will. Sometimes it was the memory of the hospital experience, the words of the nurse, the uncontrollable weeping, and the loneliness of the recovery room. Other times, I would recall the words of warning and discouragement from the people around me. There were times when I would think about my first baby. I couldn't understand why I kept thinking about it. It was over and in my past, right? There was an inner battle brewing. I would remind myself that on the night I had gone to the altar, I had told Him I was sorry for my sinful actions and the rebellious decisions. I knew that I had made so many mistakes throughout my life. I was having a hard time getting over the scars of guilt, shame, and self-condemnation. The thought of standing before the Savior completely exposed, knowing what I had done, and taking full responsibility for deliberately killing one of His little ones was more than I could bear. I knew He forgave me. But when the memory came back, I found it was too painful. The truth was I didn't know if I could ever forgive myself.

Yes, the event was in the past, but my complete healing would be in my future. Although all looked well on the outside, there was this gnawing, painful heartache I had to keep inside. But God didn't want me to live in the shadow of my past or for me to be tormented by the enemy. John 10:10 says, "The thief comes only to steal and kill and destroy; I have come that they may have life, and have it to the full" (NIV).

I knew that He forgave me and I was saved, but that was just the beginning of the healing process. He had completely and utterly forgiven me of my sins. My name was written in the Lamb's Book of Life. He was the Lord of my life. But I still needed to learn how to embrace that forgiveness. Centered in my heart was a place that held onto the guilt and shame associated with my forgiven sin. It was one thing for Him to forgive me, but it was another for me to completely let it go. The reality of my baby being more than just tissue became stronger and stronger the closer I walked with the Lord. It seemed like there was more to this sin than I had originally thought. There were times when I had to battle overwhelming feelings of shame and self-condemnation. They were always accompanied by periods of guilt. The enemy wanted to keep me tied to my past and chained to the bondage of regret.

When I looked back on the night I accepted Christ as my Savior, I began to fear that I may have only lifted up a general prayer request for forgiveness. Doubt nestled its way into my heart and became an unwanted, but it required witness to my failing faith. While my prayer for salvation was the most sincere prayer I had ever prayed at that time in my life, things had changed. I was growing in Christ and had embraced a deeper relationship with Him. The closer we got, the more intimate our relationship became, and with that intimacy came a deeper desire to be as clean and transparent with Him as possible. I didn't want anything to stand in the way of our blessed union. I knew that God was in the business of complete restoration, not a partial renovation.

It was during this season that the Lord showed me that there were some unresolved issues surrounding my abortion. He had brought me to a place where I was now ready to see His truth about that horrible experience. He wanted to show me that He had completely forgiven me and that provisions for my joyous, redeemed life had already been put into place. In order for me to totally appreciate all the Trinity had done, I needed to now forgive myself. He wanted to show me how I could receive a complete healing. He reminded me that His deepest desire was for me to live a life of healed freedom through His loving mercy. He reassured me that there was more to this than meets the eye.

In early spring that year, my church was conducting their annual Sanctity of Life service. There were speakers and videos. There were bulletin inserts with pictures of precious babies. There were articles encouraging people to volunteer at the local pregnancy center. There were appeals for donations to help girls needing baby clothes and supplies. The sermon was carefully crafted and centered on the importance of life no matter the circumstances. The unborn, the injured, the elderly—all were valuable lives to Christ. I had heard these messages in years past, but this year my heart seemed to be troubled by the message. I seemed to be more sensitive to the reference to the life of the unborn than I had been in the past. Then the pastor mentioned the word *abortion*. I'm sure he continued to talk about the forgiveness offered in Christ, but I was already being transported to the thoughts of my past. It was then I realized that those lingering feelings of shame, self-regret, and condemnation were still shrouded in the recesses of my heart. *Oh, no, here they come again! Not in church!* It was one thing for these feelings to occur in my private thoughts at night, but not while I was sitting in church on Sunday morning. The intensity of those feelings began to swell, and I was having a hard time holding back the tears. The question of whether I had been completely forgiven came to mind. How could I feel this intense regret and shame and still claim the total freedom offered in Christ? Was the Holy Spirit trying to tell me something?

Concerned that I might have some unfinished business with God, I set up an appointment to talk with my pastor. This would be the first time I mentioned this to anyone outside my family. My children and some family members had known for years. They understood, and their love and acceptance had been a blessing. But I wasn't completely sure anyone else would really understand. So with quite a bit of apprehension, but driven by my desire to be free before God, I spoke with my pastor about my past and my secret sin. Much to my relief, he was very compassionate and understanding. When he spoke, he used a gentle, soft voice. I didn't feel judged. I truly felt cared for and loved. He gave me a sense of encouragement. I was on the right path. He agreed that the Holy Spirit was guiding me to a deeper healing. He suggested I contact our local pregnancy crisis center. They had a wonderful Bible study there for women seeking a deeper healing concerning their abortions.

The following week, I met with the counselor. She was very kind and gave me a quick tour of the center. The facility was nothing fancy but was very warm and inviting. There was a kind, peaceful atmosphere here. She gave me the schedule of when the Bible study met. There was just one class, and it met in the evenings. That was convenient for me because I worked during the day. I left that evening feeling hopeful. I prayed that this would be the beginning of a journey to complete healing and freedom in Christ.

Our group was small but dedicated. We spend many weeks together. We all wanted to receive the full healing found in Christ, and we came from all walks of life. Some were young, and their experience and wounds were still fresh. Others had spent years walking the streets of regret and shame. They had learned to live with it but were dying inside.

Every week we would meet. It was a time when we could freely share our hidden pain with people who truly understood. We would begin our sessions in prayer, asking God to help reveal Himself to us through His Word. We would thank Him for His forgiveness and His Son, Jesus Christ. We asked that the Holy Spirit would minister to our hearts and heal our brokenness and wounds. We asked for the courage to open up to God and be vulnerable and transparent. We all wanted to receive His truth and mercy. The Holy Spirit seemed to hover over our special time together. It was in this loving, merciful atmosphere that we were able to freely search God's Word for the healing Scriptures that He had for us. No judgment, no condemnation, only loving compassion from an understanding heavenly Father. God was taking our damaged past and giving us a divine purpose.

We began to try to understand how we had come to make such a life-ending decision. When we understood what had truly happened, we could then specifically bring that to God for forgiveness. No longer were we going to approach this in generalities. We needed to be intentional about our request. That was the first step. We had side-stepped the issue long enough. The Holy Spirit tenderly walked us through our pasts, showing us the process of our decisions that had led to our sinful action. Each of us had different stories, different situations, but we all had the same problem: the lack of total trust in God and in His protection, provision, and purpose. In other words, we all battled with sin.

Journaling was recommended to help us concentrate on our experiences, past and present. We needed to document what the Lord was revealing so we could understand it in real terms. The notion that a fleeting thought could have lasting impact was dispelled. There was enormous power in the written word. When I took the time to stop and clearly focus on the events, thoughts, and motivations surrounding my abortion, it became clear what had happened. The choices that were made were out of my ignorance of the truth. The truth is that God loves us unconditionally. The truth is that God loves me with an everlasting love. The truth is that life begins at conception. The truth is that God would never leave me nor forsake me. The truth is that God had and has a wonderful plan for my life. Embracing these truths would have helped me to make different choices. Having these truths in my heart now allows me to embrace and trust Him at His word. Trusting God is the beginning of everything.

# *Finding God's Unfailing Love*

God always wants us to start at the beginning. For us, it was accepting the truth that God loves us unconditionally. All throughout the Bible, God repeatedly emphasizes how much He wants us to know that His love can always be obtained and trusted. His love overrides our circumstances every time. Over and over again, the Scriptures expose a love that seeks us, rescues us, and delivers us into His family. This God is truly able to love us, knowing our faults, our sins, and our rebellion. His love is stronger than our doubts, our fears, and our sins. Nothing takes Him by surprise. He is able to rescue us as we lie wounded and seeking His healing. It is so important that we see God in His true nature, holy and loving. It is only then that we are able to freely approach Him with our sin, knowing He will love us and not turn us away in disgust. He is our refuge and our answer.

Here are just a few Scriptures that reinforced that truth.

> The Lord, the Lord the compassionate and gracious God, slow to anger, abounding in love and faithfulness, maintaining love to thousands, and forgiving wickedness, rebellion and sin. (Exodus 34:6–7a NIV)

> The Lord appeared to us in the past, saying: "I have loved you with an everlasting love; I have drawn you with loving-kindness." (Jeremiah 31:3 NIV)

> But I trust in your unfailing love; my heart rejoices in your salvation. (Psalm 13:5 NIV)

> Remember, O Lord, your great mercy and love, for they are from of old. Remember not the sins of my youth and my rebellious ways; according to

> your love remember me, for you are good, O Lord. (Psalm 25:6–7 NIV)
>
> For great is your love, reaching to the heavens; your faithfulness reaches to the skies. (Psalm 57:10 NIV)
>
> I have come into the world as a light, so that no one who believes in me should stay in darkness. (John 12:46 NIV)
>
> How great is the love the Father has lavished on us, that we should be called children of God! (1 John 3:1 NIV)
>
> This is love: not that we loved God, but that he loved us and sent his Son as an atoning sacrifice for our sins. (1 John 4:10 NIV)

## Understanding Life—God's Creation

Our next step was to understand life from God's viewpoint. As Christians, we believe that life begins at conception. The moment God orchestrates the egg and seed to meet, life begins. This is a miraculous event, and the timing is always in His hands. Psalm 139:13–16 says,

> For you created my inmost being; you knit me together in my mother's womb. I praise you because I am fearfully and wonderfully made; your works are wonderful, I know that full well. My frame was not hidden from you when I was made in the secret place, when I was woven together in the depths of the earth. Your eyes saw my unformed body; all

> the days ordained for me were written in your book
> before one of them came to be. (NIV)

This scripture seems pretty straightforward concerning God's sovereign hand in the creation of life. However, when I look at my past behavior, it was evident that I tripped over this point when I was wrestling with my decision concerning my first baby. I didn't have the benefit of knowing Scripture and was left to figure it out on my own. Remember, that was when my life was being controlled by me and my limited understanding. I resorted to the world's point of view. Our world tends to focus on circumstances and situations rather than on our heavenly Father's authority. The world comes up with a variety of theories and opinions to help us navigate through this rebellious life. So it's not surprising that when I tried to understand my life's circumstances and challenges, things seemed to get a bit confusing—and in this case, deadly. Each of us had to travel our own paths. All of our aborted children's life circumstances may have begun in drastically differing ways. For some, their lives began in a marriage. For others, life began outside marriage. Some began as the result of a loving union, whereas others' lives were due to rape or incest. Many were healthy, but others had medical issues. But regardless of the surrounding circumstances, based on Scripture, their lives were created and orchestrated by God on purpose for His purpose. The children are His created blessings to us, regardless of the circumstances.

## Embracing Truth, Forgiveness, and Healing

Our weekly Bible study group continued to meet for the next few weeks. All along, we were digging deeper into our understanding of our past actions and decisions while embracing the truths found in the Word of God. I was becoming more comfortable sharing this secret with God. I knew He already knew about it, but there was something healing about openly discussing it with Him and my sisters. I had begun writing in a journal. The healing that came from writing down my feelings, recording my thoughts and questions, gave me insight and strength. Even expressing my written prayers gave me a sense of release—a letting go, if you will. What a relief. My journal entries would later give me the opportunity to go back and review the insights that the Holy Spirit had revealed and the prayers that had been crafted and answered. When I read my chronicles, it was like speaking a prayer to back to Jesus. In James 5:16, James highlights the importance of prayer with God and with one another. "Therefore confess your sins to each other and pray for each other so that you may be healed. The prayer of a righteous man is powerful and effective" (NIV).

One evening, I found myself in a particularly quiet mood. Not depressed, just quiet and listening to my heart intently. Oh, how I wanted to be healed from this sick pain in my heart. Revealing these admissions was easy at first because I was not being completely transparent; I was still holding back. My fears of shame, guilt, and condemnation were still strong. Again I searched the Scripture for some releasing answers. I remember being amazed at reading specific verses that I had known for years, but now they seemed to come alive. They really spoke to my heart in a more meaningful way. One such passage was Proverbs 3:5–6. "Trust in the Lord with all your heart and lean not on your own understanding; in all you ways acknowledge him, and he will make your paths straight" (NIV).

Trusting the Lord with all of my heart was clearly called for. That was at the center of the sin in the first place. I had only relied on me and what I could do. Now, I had to completely reverse that strategy and place my very life entirely in His hands. It was the only way to achieve complete healing and peace.

I knew that I had asked God to forgive me of my sins back in 1988, but God knew I had to go deeper. He wanted me to experience His overwhelming, unmerited forgiveness at the most profound level of all. He wanted to show me the depths of His love for me. I began to venture in to a deeper healing. This was when I needed to take the brave step and trust Him like never before. I had to accept the truth and remove the lie. I needed to come to grips with the fact that I had chosen to end a life, not remove a tissue. I could no longer run away from this. As painful and hideous as this truth was, it was the only pathway to healing. The hidden horror that I had killed my baby was at the very center of my pain. It was the nucleus, if you will, of the lingering shame and guilt. This was the concealed disgrace I was living with. It was this that I had spent years trying to hide or explain away. The consequences of the pain and devastation of my actions began to become unmistakable. The killing of this tender life had been slowly eating away at my heart. I had to embrace the reality of my baby. I had to take time to confront that very thing that I had spent years trying to sidestep, excuse, minimize, evade, and even deny. It was not a tissue—it was a beautiful child whom God had intended for life. He had created this child on purpose and for a purpose.

I knew that there would come a time when I had to stand exposed. The thought of that terrified me. How could I face Him? Even Moses hid his face from God. In the book of Exodus, it tells us, "Then he said, 'I am the God of your father, the God of Abraham, the God of Isaac and the God of Jacob.' At this, Moses hid his face, because he was afraid to look at God" (Exodus 3:6 NIV). Clearly, this was going to be a moment that I couldn't do by myself. I would need a power that was beyond my experience and understanding. I needed a power that could stand in the presence of the Almighty God and not be destroyed! In the book of Acts, it is recorded, "But you will receive power when the Holy Spirit comes on you; and you will be my witnesses in Jerusalem, and in all Judea and Samaria, and to the ends of the earth" (Acts 1:8 NIV).

Again, the power of the Holy Spirit is referenced in Ephesians when Paul is explaining how we cannot take credit for even the faith of our salvation. "For it is by grace you have been saved, through faith—and this is not from yourselves, it is the gift of God—not by works, so that no one can boast" (Ephesians 2:8–9 NIV). The power of the Holy Spirit is living inside us. We simply need to allow Him to do His work. "Guard the good deposit that was entrusted to you—guard it with the help of the Holy Spirit who lives in us" (2 Timothy 1:14 NIV).

I needed the power of the Holy Spirit! I needed Jesus *and* the Holy Spirit to stand with me in the presence of the almighty God. I envisioned Jesus standing on my right side and the Holy Spirit standing behind me, holding me up so I wouldn't faint. Jesus stood beside me, standing with me and knowing that from the beginning of time, this was my time to experience the overwhelming love, grace, and forgiveness that only comes to those who are willing to step forward in faith, believing in God's Word. He forgives all my sins and heals all my diseases (Psalm 103:3). Looking back at this moment, I can only imagine how excited and thrilled the Trinity must have been. "Look, Neva is about to see Us as We truly are for the very first time!" How they are able to turn something so hard into something so miraculous is beyond me. And miraculous it was.

I found myself entering a place that I feared the most. This was a place where I would have to meet up with the truth of my past and stand before God, transparent and without an excuse or defense. All accusations lay at His feet. The charges were read; the evidence was exposed. Guilty as charged! All I had to offer the judge in my defense was the truth of my sin and my faith that Jesus shed His blood for my sin. All I knew was that I wanted to be clean and right with Him and live the life He had for me, no matter the cost.

The stark reality of the extent of my sin was enormous. For years, I had not taken the time to examine the extensiveness of what I had done: taken a life. *Oh, God! What have I done? How can I be free from this shame? Do you still love me?* Not only had I robbed this child of a life on earth, but I had also robbed the rest of the world from sharing that life. I could no longer shy away from this harsh reality. *Forgive me, Lord! Oh, Lord! Please forgive me!*

As my traumatized body shook and the healing tears fell down my weary face, the Lord began to soothe my heart and calm my fears. I became aware that there was a sweet atmosphere filling the room. There was a holy hush that seemed to fall over me. That was when I heard Him gently whispering in my ear, "Neva, remember that We've got this. We have always had this. Not only your life and your soul; but We also have your baby. We have had her from the very moment you released her. At the very moment of her death on earth, she was delivered whole and beautiful into Our loving, caring, and divine arms. We have always sought for you to be united with her."

The moment was overwhelming. I tried to grasp what was being revealed. *My baby is alive? My baby is with you? How can that be? Oh, my! Could it be true?* It had never occurred to me that my child would be alive. Hope began to fill my heart. I realized that during the entire time of my years of torment, I had only been focusing on the death of my child. This was another example of the pitfalls of relying on my limited understanding.

Looking back, I had not thoroughly understood the Scriptures that spoke about death and heaven. I had certainly never applied them to my baby's death. God reminded me of 2 Corinthians 5:8, where Paul talks about it being better to be with the Lord and absent from our bodies: To be absent from the body is to be present in the Lord. And in 1 Thessalonians 4:13–18, Paul writes that those who are dead will be with Christ when He returns. It became clear. Oh, how marvelous, how amazing! Because I was willing to fully embrace my child's death, Christ was eager to completely reveal His truth about life. What hope! What encouragement! Did I dare entertain thoughts of life concerning my child?

My mind and my heart were racing. I found myself imagining what my little one's life would be like. I allowed myself to feel the tiny body nestled in my arms. I could see the baby's eyes and beautiful smiling lips.

Then came an amazing moment that I will never forget. I noticed that as I was looking at my baby, I saw Them out of the corner of my eye. There they were—Father, Son, and the Holy Spirit. I had a sense that They were standing there, watching me, watching us. I noticed a soft, compassionate expression on Jesus's face. It was such a tender moment. They seemed to be smiling at me as though They had been waiting for this moment for years. "Wait a minute! Did you say *her*? My baby is a girl? I have a daughter?" The joy was indescribable, unspeakable, and beyond anything I had ever experienced! They revealed the beautiful creation They had given me so many years ago. Oh, how wonderfully made she was! In that moment, the fire of their all-surpassing love immediately consumed all of my guilt, shame, and pain right before my eyes. All the horror of my actions was burned up in the intense flame of Their love. Out of my grief, He gave me life! He turned beauty from ashes, my mourning to praise.

> To all who mourn in Israel, he will give a crown of beauty for ashes, a joyous blessing instead of mourning, festive praise instead of despair. In their righteousness, they will be like great oaks that the LORD has planted for his own glory. (Isaiah 61:3 NLT)

> And we know that in all things God works for the good of those who love him, who have been called according to his purpose. (Romans 8:28 NIV)

> Praise be to the God and Father of our Lord Jesus Christ, who has blessed us in the heavenly realms with every spiritual blessing in Christ. For he chose us in him before the creation of the world to be holy and blameless in his sight. In love, he predestined us to be adopted as his sons through Jesus Christ, in accordance with his pleasure and will—to the praise of his glorious grace, which he has freely given us

> in the One he loves. In him we have redemption through his blood, the forgiveness of sins, in accordance with the riches of God's grace that he lavished on us with all wisdom and understanding. (Ephesians 1:3–8 NIV)

When I look back at that moment, I now see that there had been a purpose and a provision for all of my pain and suffering. He had truly kept me. In Isaiah 38:17, the prophet Isaiah tells us, "Surely it was for my benefit that I suffered such anguish. In your love you kept me from the pit of destruction; you have put all my sins behind your back" (NIV). When He put my sins behind his back, He also puts them out of sight, out of reach, out of mind, and out of existence.

I understand the new truth: the Lord wastes nothing. All of my life was going to be used as a testimony to reveal the magnificent grace and love offered to us. He gave me a testimony revealing the redeemed life of those who follow Him. His predestined plan for my life was perfect. My life was wonderfully made! What an amazing God!

## Releasing Our Babies

At the end of our Bible study class, we had all been given the marvelous gift of self-forgiveness. We all had become acquainted with our babies. During our last evening session, we were asked to take time to give our children their names. It was an important step of finally recognizing their existence and their lives. I didn't have any trouble knowing her name: Julianne. I knew that the moment I laid spiritual eyes on her. Thank You, Jesus! The realization that she was alive and living with the Trinity was such a remarkably wonderful blessing. No longer did I feel the guilt and shame associated with her death. Because of Their amazing love, I was now able to see the truth surrounding my daughter's life. I had spent so many years relying on my own understanding of that event that I had been totally unaware of the reality of God's authority and plan over it. He took my rebellion and used it to show me His overarching love. All that was required of me to experience this abundant blessing was for me to totally surrender to Him and ask for His specific forgiveness. It was at that very moment of surrender that He revealed His truth. Now I have the eternal blessing of her life. I can now call her out in prayer by name. I can love her tenderly knowing that she is safe and well. Her life did have a purpose, and her life will be shared by others!

At the end of the evening, we had a ceremony to symbolize our children's release back into our heavenly Father's arms. We all knew that someday we would be united with our precious little ones in Christ. Oh, what a wonderful day that will be! Until then, they were all in His amazing care. These children, who were never born in sin, anxiously await our eternal lives together in heaven. While releasing balloons into the evening sky, we prayed again, thanking Jesus for His sacrifice, the Holy Spirit for His comfort, and God the Father for His sovereign plan. All our children have known is the Father and the Son and the Holy Spirit. That is the best family anyone could ask for.

# Insights from My Journal

I want to highlight some of the key insights that came from my journaling experience. Some have already been mentioned but are worth repeating.

I began to journal my thoughts and the truths of His Word. My journal quickly filled up with countless healing truths found in the Bible. I found that when I recorded what He was saying and what I was learning, there was a sense of release and relief in it. I was able to talk to God by writing down my thoughts. Our conversations had real meaning and substance. Not only did I believe that He heard me, but I was able to hear Him. As time went on, journaling allowed me to go back and revisit and review what He was showing me. In doing so, it reinforced the truths that He was revealing. Nothing was a passing thought, no shifting sand. Every word became concrete truths that I could stand on and call upon. He walked me through the journey of my life. My heart was slowly healing. Truth by truth, scripture by scripture, my wounds were being replaced by His Word. The healing salve of the Word was being applied every time I read a verse.

I slowly began to understand the nature of my sin and His boundless, loving forgiveness. With that new understanding, I was able to find countless examples where God extends mercy, grace, forgiveness, and complete healing.

There are so many places where God makes His love and mercy known to us. There are places where He shows us that He will never leave us or forsake us. I would review and uncover the depths of my sin while He wanted me to see how magnificent and loving His ways are. It was then that I found both the depths of His love and the wretchedness of my heart. He gave me a new understanding of my sin nature. He was able to clean and purify my heart like never before.

I found that there are many places in the Bible where the importance of having a clean heart before God matters. I was drawn to the story about David and how he so terribly turned away from God and behaved in selfish rebellion, taking his life into his own hands. In the story, David had committed a multitude of sins, two of which were adultery and murder. His need to fulfill his desires at all costs and then cover up his actions seemed to resonate within my heart. I began to understand that the condition of the sinful human heart is universal. Now, in this story, David is confronted with his actions. At the realization of what he had done in God's eyes, he was overtaken with grief. He began imploring the Lord to grant mercy and compassion. He pleaded with God to wash away all his iniquity and cleanse him of his sin. What struck me about this story was that David had been serving God for years, and yet he still found himself in a place of rebellion and selfishness. He had already dedicated his life to serve God, but the element of sinful desires still had a place in his heart. I realized that it isn't until we see our actions in light of God's perception that we can truly begin the healing process. When the hideousness of his action was made clear to him, David wrote, "Create in me a clean heart, O God, and renew a steadfast spirit within me" (Psalm 51:10 NIV).

I could really relate. In the book of Psalms, David implores the Lord, "Search me, God, and know my heart; test me and know my anxious thoughts. See if there is any offensive way in me, and lead me in the way everlasting" (Psalm 139:23–24 NIV).

God reveals in His Word that we can have a clean heart. His desire for an intimate relationship with us is breathtaking. The more I searched Him and who He is, the more I understood the vastness of His love sacrifice for me. The Lord had begun to lay a foundation of love and trust in my life. For the first nine years, He filled me with His Word and loved me faithfully. It was on that foundation that He began to heal me. As time went on, I found myself able to understand why I had begun to be more and more preoccupied with memories of my abortion. My journaling helped me comprehend why I didn't experience anything radical at first, just brief moments of recollection and reflection. As I mentioned before, sometimes it was the memory of the hospital experience, the words of the nurse, the uncontrollable weeping, and the loneliness of the recovery room.

Other times, I would recall the facial expressions and tone of voices of those people around me that gave me words of discouragement and warning. I began to understand why I kept thinking about it. It was over, in my past, right? Yes, the event was in the past, but my complete healing would be in my future. There were scars of betrayal, guilt, and shame that had to be dealt with. The thought of standing quietly and being exposed before the Savior, knowing what I had done, and taking full responsibility for deliberately killing one of His little ones was more than I could bear. I knew that it was too painful and didn't know what to do. While all looked well on the outside, there was this gnawing, ugly secret I had to keep inside.

I recorded my memories of the Sundays when my church would celebrate Sanctity of Life as being the most difficult. Listening to all the anti-abortion, pro-life comments caused such conflicting emotions within me. I had come to understand the truth about life beginning at conception. There was no denying that, but how could I be free from the guilt I felt associated with my past? I was living a wonderful Christian life on the outside. Believe me, no one would have ever suspected my past. But God didn't want me to live in the shadow of my past or for me to be tormented by the enemy. John 10:10 says, "The thief comes only to steal and kill and destroy; I have come that they may have life, and have it to the full" (NIV). It was becoming more and more apparent that I needed to address this hidden secret from His point of view, not justifying it with the excuse of keeping vows and honoring my husband. So, trusting Him and His Word, I began to journal to help me seek His forgiveness. I had to slow down long enough and stop running from the inevitable moment I must have with Him. Now that I saw what I had done through His eyes, and not through the eyes of someone trying to justify and rationalize the abortion for my convenience and selfish desires, I was drawn into a place that I had never experienced before. I don't know that I had ever really seen sin as disgusting and offensive to Him before.

I noted that as I looked back, it seemed that all of my other sins that I had brought before Him were bad and that those sins needed His forgiveness, but this one was more than I could handle. It was almost like this time, when I told Him I was sorry and asked Him for forgiveness, I really couldn't see how He could. How could He forgive something so horrible? Again, I was trying to capture His infinite loving forgiveness with a finite mind. As I journaled, I discovered that He was taking me to a place where only trust could lead me. It seemed that the other sins like lying, gossip, not loving Him more, slander, and slowness to forgive others seemed to be sins that just disappointed Him. You know, like when I would misbehave as a child, I would tell my mom I was sorry. She would always bend down, give me a kiss, and say, "It's okay, honey. Just don't do it again." But this sin, well, I just couldn't see how anyone would be able to forgive it, much less the Creator of the universe. He couldn't just say, "It's okay, honey. Just don't do it again." I just couldn't see how He could do that! But you see, that's the thing about His blood and the cross. The sacrifice He made, the blood He shed for me, wasn't just for those times when He picked me up after I stubbed my toe or tripped over a pebble. It was also for the times when I needed Him to rescue me from the darkest pit, the fiery furnace, the places that no one but the God of the universe can preside over and conquer. "Trust in the Lord with all your heart, and lean not on your own understanding. In all your ways acknowledge Him in all your ways and He will direct your paths" (Proverbs 3:5–6 NIV).

My journaling prepared me for the moment when I had to stand exposed. The thought of being so vulnerable before the Lord was beyond anything I could imagine. I poured out my heart filled with fear. The pages were wet with my tears as I wrote my thoughts. How could I face Him? As mentioned before, even Moses hid his face from God. The book of Exodus tells us, "Then he said, 'I am the God of your father, the God of Abraham, the God of Isaac and the God of Jacob.' At this, Moses hid his face, because he was afraid to look at God" (Exodus 3:6 NIV). An encounter of this magnitude was going to be a moment that I couldn't do by myself.

I would clearly need a power that was beyond my experience and understanding. I needed a power that could stand in the presence of the almighty God and not be destroyed! In the book of Acts, it is recorded, "But you will receive power when the Holy Spirit comes on you; and you will be my witnesses in Jerusalem, and in all Judea and Samaria, and to the ends of the earth" (Acts 1:8 NIV).

Again, the power of the Holy Spirit is referenced in Ephesians when Paul is explaining how we cannot take credit for even the faith of our salvation. "For it is by grace you have been saved, through faith—and this is not from yourselves, it is the gift of God—not by works, so that no one can boast" (Ephesians 2:8–9 NIV). The power of the Holy Spirit is living inside us. We simply need to allow Him to do His work. Second Timothy 1:14 states, "Guard the good deposit that was entrusted to you—guard it with the help of the Holy Spirit who lives in us" (NIV). I needed the power of the Holy Spirit! I needed Jesus *and* the Holy Spirit to stand with me in the presence of God.

The power of journaling gave me the opportunity to slow down and examine my thoughts and fears. It also allowed me time to search His Word for better understanding and direction. I can't emphasis enough the potency of the journaling phenomenon. It gave me an intentionality and focus that I had never experienced before. So much of my past experience had been dealing with fleeting thoughts or passing emotions. But when I took time to write them down, I was able to examine them and see them in a more rational light. The confusion and the fog began to lift, and I was able to more clearly see what God was telling and showing me. And over time, my recorded journey became an amazing reminder of what He revealed. It developed into a testimony, a living confirmation of His wonderful power, love, and enduring faithfulness in my life. It is a clear witness that I rely on to this day. Here are a few verses that reinforce the truth of our Lord's faithfulness.

God is not a man, that He should lie, Nor a son of man, that He should change His mind. Does He speak and then not act? Does He promise and not fulfill? (Numbers 23:29 NIV)

Your faithfulness continues through all generations; you have established the earth, and it endures. (Psalm 119:90 NIV)

But the Lord is faithful, and He will strengthen and protect you from the evil one. (2 Thessalonians 3:3 NIV)

Let us hold unswervingly to the hope we profess, for He who promised is faithful. (Hebrews 10:23 NIV)

# My Testimonial Journey

So there you have it. My life's testimony, written in obedience to what God has called me to write. A life that, by the world's standards, was unremarkable and uninteresting. Born in the Midwest, grew up, lived on a farm, attended college, married, had children, divorced. It was nothing unusual, nothing wonderful, just a run-of-the-mill life. But based on God's standards, there couldn't be anything further from the truth. The truth is my entire life is wonderfully made before the beginning of creation of the world.

Ephesians 1:4 declares, "For he chose us in him before the creation of the world to be holy and blameless in his sight. In love he predestined us to be adopted as his sons through Jesus Christ, in accordance with his pleasure and will" (NIV). The moment I accepted Christ into my life, I was able to embrace this amazing truth. He continues to reveal His beauty in my life daily!

My life is wonderfully made! Now, I have to admit when I began this testimonial journey, I would not have intentionally put those five words together. However, that is the power of journaling your testimony. God will continue to reveal Himself to you in new ways as you seek Him. True to form, God's ways are not our ways. In Isaiah, we are reminded of how magnificent our God's ways truly are. In chapter 55, verses 6 - 9, we are invited to see the truth of our mighty God: "Seek the Lord while he may be found; call on him while he is near. Let the wicked forsake his way and the evil man his thoughts. Let Him turn to the Lord, and he will have mercy on him, and to our God, for he will freely pardon. For my thoughts are not your thoughts, neither are your ways my ways," declares the Lord. "As the heavens are higher than the earth so are my ways higher than your ways and my thoughts than your thoughts" (NIV).

I have lived in the wonderful freedom of His forgiveness for many years now. I have been able to walk in the presence of God, knowing that I am forgiven and cleansed by the blood of His Son, Jesus Christ. Abundant peace and joy have entered my life. I have learned that God doesn't waste anything and uses all of our lives to show others who He is and what He has done for us. I know that my daughter is alive and in heaven waiting for our marvelous reunion. I learned that we cannot fathom God's riches. The mystery of how He turns something horrible into something that glorifies Him is astounding. My life has been forever changed because of this love. They (Father, Son, and Holy Spirit) seek to have an intimate relationship with all of us, no matter our past.

God has continued to bless my life in many ways. One of the most magnificent ways is that I have been given a husband who loves me and loves the Lord. I am blessed by his daily understanding and encouragement. He has walked this journey with me with loving and remarkable support. His heart has reflected Jesus's love and passion for the healing truths given to us in the Word. He understands the importance of this testimony. He prays for those who will be encouraged and moved to seek God's amazing forgiveness. Our hearts are united and filled with the love for those wounded and seeking true healing. Thank You, Jesus!

I'm also abundantly blessed with amazing children and grandchildren, all of whom have remarkable calls on their lives. God has marked them all for greatness. He reveals this truth to me daily. Their lives will be a testament to our Lord's great mercy and grace. Watching them as they navigate life's journey has been one of the greatest joys in my life. God never fails to enter in and use their life lessons to move them to new places and understandings. To God be the glory.

I'm also blessed to serve God through our church. I'm serving Him in our choir, drama, food pantry, missions, and Sunday school class, teaching the Word weekly. All of these blessings have given me a great opportunity to share the love of Christ with others. I have had some wonderful experiences of sharing Christ and watching others come to know His saving grace. And while all of this has been amazingly wonderful, there has been a sense that there was more that He had for me. I've continue putting one foot in front of the other, walking with Him, and seeking His face and direction for my life. Now I'm abundantly clear that His purpose for me during this season of my life is to share this incredible experience of His healing forgiveness with others who are tormented with the guilt and shame associated with their abortion. Freedom is yours!

I believe that the visions He has given me have changed me in ways beyond my understanding. The moment the Trinity loved me in the courtroom, the manifestation of Their perfect provision when They revealed the truth about Julianne, was given to me so that others would see Their compassion and Their personal involvement in our lives. Most of all, my greatest lesson was the everlasting truth that comes from heaven's throne:

**You are wonderfully made.**
**Don't worry, Neva. We've got this!**

# Receive the Free Gift Walking in Truth

Those of us who have experienced this life-changing event have had a roller coaster of emotions. There was the suffocating fear of being found out and judged harshly by friends and family. There was the convincing doubt that there would never be any forgiveness available for us and the hideous torment of self-condemnation. We feverishly sought the temporary relief that was provided in the shroud of denial in which we cloaked ourselves. Not surprisingly, this was frequently followed by our fear of ridicule and condemnation whenever the topic raised its head. Then there were the episodes of the substantial disbelief of ever being able to be free of the horrible memories. This was all followed by the recurring feelings of condemnation and self-loathing associated with such cowardice. This was always accompanied by the fear and shame that continuously loitered in the shadows of our souls. What a roller coaster ride it has been! It seemed like it would never end; it would be a continuous journey of regret and secret condemnation. How could I ever be right again, whole again? How could I face God, knowing what I did? I found myself grasping onto the only hope I could find, that of the truths found in Scripture: "There is no condemnation for those who are in Christ Jesus." "He that began a good work in you will be faithful to complete it onto the day of Jesus Christ." "Yet while we were still sinners, Christ died for us." These verses and many more were a true comfort. They all spoke to the magnificent power of God. But they all contained one very important element needed to receive the amazing healing comfort they provided—faith.

Although I always fancied myself as being a positive person, someone who would try to find the good in bad situations and give people the benefit of the doubt, when it came to this topic in my life, I still found myself floundering at believing that a holy God would never forgive such an unholy act.

How could I wrap my mind around this fundamental gift of grace in light of my sin? But you see, that is the very crux of the issue of grace. It is, by definition, the unmerited favor of God. The key word is *unmerited*! There is no way I could ever earn grace. There are no achievements needed to obtain, no successes to accomplish, no failures to correct; there is nothing that I can do to warrant His merciful grace. The only part I play in this is to accept it, embrace it, and believe it. It is truly the simple act of receiving—receiving a gift that was prepared specifically for me. The giver of this gift is the person of Jesus Christ. He not only is the lover of my soul, but He is the one who bore the cost of this gift, the gift of unconditional love. Knowing all about me, my sin, my choices, my failures, and my desires, in light of all that,

**Jesus loves me because He does.**
**It is just that simple.**

These Scriptures were written for me. Now I must walk in their truth. That would mean I would need to remind myself of this new truth every time the old thoughts of condemnation would flood my mind. I must indulge in the relentless pursuit of His truth, constantly seeking His wisdom and what He has given me, learning about the love He has for me. The Bible says that if I seek God, He will be found and make Himself known. In the book of James, first chapter, it talks about seeking God's wisdom and how He is faithful to reveal Himself to us. But there is a catch: you must believe and not doubt.

If any of you lacks wisdom, he should ask God, who gives generously to all without finding fault, and it will be given to him. But when he asks, he must believe and not doubt, because he who doubts is like a wave of the sea, blown and tossed by the wind. That man should not think he will receive anything from the Lord; he is a double-minded man, unstable in all he does. (James 1:5–8 NIV)

"Like a wave of the sea, blown and tossed by the wind"—that was my roller coaster! I was missing the power of believing! I wasn't letting go and giving God the opportunity to show me that I was made new. You see, He wants us to receive this wisdom and grace. So I must baptize myself in this reality daily.

To be baptized is to be submersed completely. It is a term used in the dyeing of cloth. Dyers would take a cloth and drench it in a bath of dye. When the cloth was saturated, they would remove it from the water, and every fiber of the cloth would then retain the new color. Truly made new! It no longer looked like it had before it was baptized in the dye. That is what happened to me when I was able to embrace God's grace. I was truly a new creature in Christ.

> Therefore, if anyone is in Christ, he is a new creation; old things have passed away; behold, all things have become new. Now all things are of God, who has reconciled us to Himself through Jesus Christ, and has given us the ministry of reconciliation, that is, that God was in Christ reconciling the world to Himself, not imputing their trespasses to them, and has committed to us the word of reconciliation. (2 Corinthians 5:17–19 NKJV)

The final part of the process of forgiveness is remembering to embrace the full truth of the Gospel of Jesus Christ. That incorporates the confession of sin, the request for forgiveness, the acceptance of that forgiveness, and then walking in the freedom of that forgiveness. Not just thanking Him for what He did but embracing the new life that it gives us. Merely thanking Him is the mental part, but then embracing the newness this forgiveness offers us is the heart of this amazing forgiveness. That is where your ability to forgive yourself originates. This begins a journey of new thinking and believing.

Old, habitual thinking and responses need to be challenged every time they reappear. It's important to embrace the forgiveness and then take every thought that comes to mind and is contrary to our new truth. Christ has forgiven us, and our redemption is immediate. The patterns and experiences and reactions to that old sin are habits that no longer have any place in our lives. They have been going on for years, and so the flesh needs to take time to embrace this new truth of being forgiven. Now, you can embrace the forgiveness immediately and are redeemed immediately, but then as you walk in that, you need to walk boldly, taking every thought captive and not going back to the thoughts of condemnation, guilt, and shame. You need to remind yourself what Christ did for you on the cross every day. As time goes on, those old thoughts of self-condemnation turn into thoughts of praise and worship.

Finally, I had the answer I was looking for. How did I get off the roller coaster of shame? How did I step onto the firm foundation of a new life, a life saturated in true freedom of the forgiveness of my secret sin? It is accomplished by seeking His Word, accepting His forgiveness, and walking in that truth daily. The Scripture of 2 Chronicles 7:14 comes to mind: "If my people who are called by my name will humble themselves, and pray and seek my face, and turn from their wicked ways, then will I hear from heaven, and will forgive their sin and will heal their land" (NKJV).

My life at the end of the ride did not end up in a life that was shadowed in shame. It actually became a life that was enlightened in forgiveness and healing. For the Lord seeks to heal, and He seeks to forgive. His purpose for our lives is to live with Him, worship Him, praise Him, and enjoy the blessings He has for us. Amazingly, that only comes through the saving forgiveness that is offered to us through Jesus Christ. This is true, complete forgiveness. We have freedom from the bondage of sin that so entraps our hearts. We are now given lives to live without the shame and despair from our past. We are transformed into lives of joy and celebration and hope and encouragement. For God loves us so much that He gave His only begotten son that whosoever believes in him will not perish but have eternal life (John 3:16 NIV). "Will not perish," "will not perish," "will not perish"—those words took on a whole new meaning after Christ's healing of my baby's abortion. For my baby, she perished at my hand, at my decision. She died in the midst of my fear and desperation, of my selfishness and self-centeredness. How can I live a life of joy and peace and celebration when it is shadowed in the knowledge of such traumatic and devastating actions? Well, that is the purpose of this book.

The purpose of this book is to share the truth of not only my sin, not only the sin that shrouded my heart, and not only the confusion and the fear and denial. It is meant to show the forgiveness, openness, and freedom that I've experienced when God came into my life and showed me how He forgave me and has provided. Not only has He forgiven me, but He has now given me a voice. I have a voice to speak of my child and the children in heaven. I've been given a voice to celebrate God's provision in our lives. To be absent from the body is to be present in the Lord (2 Corinthians 5:8). Again, the Word reassures us. Paul is speaking about those who die in 1 Thessalonians 4:13. He states, "Brothers, we do not want you to be ignorant about those who fall asleep or to grieve like the rest of men, who have no hope" (NIV). God has given me the revelation of our children's well-being, security, comfort, and happiness. You see, at the very moment of their deaths on earth, they were delivered whole and beautiful into the arms of the loving, caring, and forgiving God. He is a God who seeks for you to be united with the loved one that you so desperately love, even today in your private thoughts.

Jesus was the one who directed me to the Father, and the Holy Spirit encouraged me to go. Jesus was the way to the truth and the life, and the Holy Spirit was the fire and encouragement. It was in this power I was able to experience and enjoy Jesus. He was directing me to the relationship with the holy, mighty God of the universe—Father God.

God wastes nothing! He uses it all! He uses our sins, our failures, our shortcomings—He uses it all. According to Ezekiel 36:33, "This is what the Sovereign Lord says: 'On the day I cleanse you from all your sins, I will resettle your towns, and the ruins will be rebuilt'" (NIV).

# Purpose of This Book

Now that I have shared my testimony and my thoughts, let me take a few moments and share with you what I believe is the true purpose of this book. Quite frankly, it is you. I don't know you personally, but I do believe I know you spiritually. The reason why you decided to pick up this book may have been an intentional act on your part, or maybe it comes to you as an unexpected surprise. Either way, I am absolutely convinced that it was the result of you responding to the prompting of the Holy Spirit.

Frankly, the topic of this book is not a comfortable one. It was not intended to be light reading. Abortion is often seen as a topic not to be openly discussed, and it's a very controversial issue. In the past few decades, it has become a highly debated political topic that carries much passion and fervor. Some believe it is too sensitive to talk about or too private an experience to share. In some circles, it may even be seen as one of the unmentionable sins. That particular sin that no one wants to address. This secret sin is so secret that it isn't even one of the sins that are revealed when people testify about God's deliverance and forgiveness in their lives. I don't ever remember hearing an open testimony from anyone about how God released them from the emotional and spiritual consequences of abortion. The key word here is *open*. I have had women confide in me about their experiences, but it isn't ever a discussion that is shared by others.

It seems that when we look at sins that involve what may be perceived to be unnatural or unthinkable, we are more likely to not discuss them. They are too difficult to grasp, too hard to understand, too horrible to extend the hand of grace. For some, it may be easier to judge, condemn, or write off as unforgivable. So we try to navigate through this journey, relying on our own understanding and reasoning. We may try to attempt to deal with it by compartmentalizing and prioritizing the sin. By this I mean that concerning some sins, we may have identified them as understandable, whereas we may have determined that others are wretched and outside the limits of forgiveness and grace. We may find ourselves blaming those people who we believe were the direct perpetrators of the sin. Predictably, when it comes to the sin of abortion, the focused attention has been on the person we see as the obvious transgressor, the woman. We assume that she alone must be the one who is responsible for making that life-ending, sinful decision. The attention and blame has been placed on her because it is sometimes easier to tie the sin directly to a sinner. And though it is true that ending a life is a sin, we may have overlooked the far-reaching extent to which the abortion decision has provoked others to engage in sinful behavior as well. There were lives that judged her, hearts that were cruel to her, family and friends who abandoned her. There is such an extensive trail of damaged lives. So many people have been injured by this grim decision. As difficult as it was for the mother to go through with the abortion, there were many others who walked the path alongside her. All need healing and need to receive the grace, love, and forgiveness offered by Jesus Christ.

Unfortunately, grace and compassion may not be our first impulses. Apparently, the thought that someone would intentionally end innocent life can be beyond our ability to easily understand. There is a stigma attached to this sin, and we don't know how to process it. No surprise that we have had a hard time addressing it openly!

But this book is not about judging people. It is, however, about revealing the powerful, life-changing forgiveness, grace, and abounding love for everyone found in our Lord and Savior Jesus Christ.

Certainly, the level of grace needed here is far beyond our normal abilities and inclinations. This requires a *supernatural, sacrificial intervention*. I once heard a pastor speak about how grace was messy and that the cross was messy too. There is nothing clean and tidy at the foot of the cross. It is wretched, bloody, and deadly. This is the perfect description of our secret sin. Regardless of what we call it—procedure, abortion, or choice—if you have experienced it firsthand, you know about how it alters your life in unexpected ways. We have had to deal with that paralyzing moment when, even at the casual mention of abortion, we once again relive the cruelty of the event. For a brief moment, that cleverly suppressed memory bursts forth in total recall and shuts us down. We find may ourselves in a quagmire of emotions, followed by an overwhelming desire to run and hide for fear of being exposed. We suffer our shame and guilt and find ourselves experiencing our own personal crucifixion. If, however, you have experienced it on the sidelines, then you are reminded of the turmoil, pain, fear, shame and confusion that surrounded that difficult time. In all instances, we are all left with an overwhelming state of humiliation and guilt. This unwelcome reminder has, once again, chiseled another scar into our hearts. Emotional and spiritual freedom seems to be outside our grasp. Healing looks as if it is impossible.

It is serious business, this forgiveness and grace that Jesus spoke about. Can it really apply to *all* sins, to all sinners? Is His blood really that strong?

I'm reminded of the story in John 8 about the woman caught in adultery. She had been judged guilty of sin and was sentenced to be stoned to death. Jesus, understanding the far-reaching tentacle of sin, addresses this issue in His statement: "If anyone of you is without sin, let him be the first to throw a stone at her" (John 8:7 NIV).

In verse 4, the leaders wanted to know how Jesus would judge her sin. In our current lives, we are still asking that same question: "What do you say, Jesus?" Jesus made it very clear that none of us are without sin, as revealed in John 8:7. We are also reminded of God's assessment of our hearts' condition in Romans 3:23, which tell us, "For all have sinned and fall short of the glory of God" (NIV). We all need Jesus's forgiveness.

But before we can receive our forgiveness and embrace the complete release from our sin that is offered in Christ Jesus, we must first acknowledge that we have sin.

In approaching this topic, I began to think about all the different people who may be seeking healing and forgiveness. There were three groups of people that quickly came to mind. There were those who were complicit, those who were condemning, and those who were unaware. All three of these categories carry a wounded burden needing God's healing as the result of their involvement.

But there was a fourth group. In this group were the people who loved the woman, understood her, and recognized the cunning deception with which she was dealing. They spent countless hours praying for her, seeking God for wisdom and discernment on how to help her, asking the Father to give her mercy, and travailing for her in the altar and at the foot of the cross. These people understood the truth of God's love, mercy, and grace. They embraced Romans 3:23. They knew that Jesus offers His love freely to each and every one of us. They understood the true cost of standing in the gap. Clearly, their lives have also been changed.

Bottom line:, in all groups, the trajectory of individual lives has been altered. That small child, that decision, that single moment in time has touched them all profoundly.

In these few pages, I pray that you were able to embrace the opportunity to settle this in your life and finally, once and for all, understand and acknowledge for yourself how you can be free of the burden you may have as the result of your abortion experience. Whether you were the mother, father, relative, friend, or prayer warrior, Jesus eagerly wants to give you His peace and reveal the healing truths that the Holy Spirit has for you in the confident hope that you too will find the peace that passes all understanding, and that you will see the truth through God's eyes and receive the serenity that you so desperately seek.

It is important to note that I do not carry a degree on this subject from an institution of higher learning, I don't profess to be a global expert on the topic, and I haven't attempted to address this from a sociopolitical position. I have, however, shared with you my personal testimony as a woman who underwent a life-changing abortion and received the all-encompassing power of forgiveness from the loving Savior. This level of forgiveness resulted in a joyously free and healed life. I have also highlighted some of the insights He gave me concerning my aborted daughter in heaven, all of which, I believe, have come directly from the precious voices in heaven, the Holy Spirit and Julianne. They have spoken clearly to me on what they want you to know by revealing Scripture and supplying me with the courage to share my testimony.

My prayer now is that you embrace this life-changing journey to complete healing and begin to live the abundant life of which the Savior speaks:

> The thief comes only to steal and kill and destroy; I have come that they may have life, and have it to the full. (John 10:10 NIV)

# Julianne's Letters from Heaven

I struggled with the thought of whether I should include the following section. I wasn't sure whether I should reveal such private encounters that I have had with my daughter in heaven. But the Holy Spirit revealed to me, during the Come to the Garden Retreat, that the messages she had for me were also for all the mothers who have had or are suffering with the brokenness of their loss. These children are part of the healing message God has for us, and I was meant to share them. I refer to them as my Letters from Heaven. These are some of the thoughts, encouragements, and insights that Julianne has given me over the years. I was to release them into His care and allow Him to do His work in the hearts of the readers.

Her comments and prayer shine the light on the reality of their lives in heaven. Her sweet voice so tenderly whispers a message of comfort, love, and encouragement. The moments we have shared over the past years have been amazing. They have been the result of my complete healing. They were revealed to me during my journal writing. They have been revealed during my quiet times in my prayer closet. And most recently, they have been revealed during my daily walks. They have truly been special blessings that the Lord has given me. These entries are a reflection of our special time together. Some people may not understand how such conversations could take place with someone who has passed on. Well, believe me, these are thoughts, impressions, and words of encouragement that could never have come into being if not for the miraculous touch of the Holy Spirit. So with that in mind, and with the tender heart of my daughter, may you be blessed with the insights she shares from heaven.

***

*Mom, I never left you. I was always with you. The moment you allowed the doctor to perform the surgery (or the procedure, if you will), I was always with you. What you didn't know, Mom, was that the moment I was released from you, God received me into His arms.*

*Scripture refers to how wonderful it is "To be away from the body and at home with the Lord" (2 Corinthians 5:8 NIV). I have been with Him ever since then. Amazingly, the moment of your loss was the moment of my eternal birth. What God intends to be created, no man can separate. "So, they are no longer two, but one flesh. Therefore, what God has joined together, let no one separate" (Matthew 19:6 NIV). He tells us that in His Word. This verse applies to all His created things! So even though you thought we were separated, we were actually joined eternally. You thought that I was dead. But that was never God's purposed plan for my life. His purposed plan for my life was for me to spend eternity with Him. He created me! He allowed me to be conceived! "I praise you because I am fearfully and wonderfully made; your works are wonderful, I know that full well" (Psalm 139:14 NIV).*

*From the beginning of time, He also had a desired plan for me. That desired plans was for me to live with you and for you to bring me up. He wanted me to have a life on earth with you. He wanted me to grow up and learn about Him. He wanted me to share His love with others and to encourage others in His love.*

*But then the battle began, the battle between His purposed and desired will for my life. It is important to know that nothing can supersede the purposed will of God. Because you have a free will, you chose to choose the desire of your heart instead of God's. However, God's purpose will prevail. Although I understand that your choice focused on you, on your pleasures, on your convenience, and on what you thought you could handle, God's sovereign, purposed plan for my life was to be fulfilled. And although you were completely oblivious to this universal truth, He was going to have His way. So the life He wanted for me developed into an incredible life from heaven.*

*I know you have spent countless hours wondering what my life's purpose was. What would I have been like in elementary school, junior high school, and high school? Would I play well with others? Would I be pretty? What color hair would I have? Would I have a giggle or laugh? I know you have asked these questions. You wanted to know what my life would have been like had I gone through the full-term pregnancy and been delivered into your world. Well, God had that all planned out. He has always had a higher purpose for me. That's why He allowed, in His sovereign will and His lovingkindness, for me to be delivered into heaven. Because the moment I was delivered into heaven, I was given the amazing purpose of my life: to praise Him and lift Him up, to worship Him and adore Him, to learn about His marvelous works, to experience how great He is, and to understand the purpose He has for you and me. It was to know Him, share His love with others, and encourage others and live with Him for eternity. This was all fulfilled.*

*My purpose was you. My purpose was to let you know how wonderful God is and that even in light of your sin, He still loves you, He loves me, and He prepared a way for us to be reunited one day, for us to have a life together for eternity together in heaven. Because you see, He understands the heartache and heartbreak as the result of the decision you made. He knew how difficult it was to embrace the lie from the enemy, desperately trying to convince yourself that I wasn't human, that I wasn't a divine creation, but that I was nothing more than an inconvenient accumulation of cells, that I wasn't anything more than tissue. That was the lie from the pit of hell.*

*Praise God—the eternal truth is that the lie from the enemy is never stronger than the love from the Lord. He knew that He created you, and He created me. He ensured that we are fearfully and wonderfully made for a divine purpose on purpose.*

*Oh, Mom, I can't thank you enough for seeking forgiveness, embracing the truth, and taking the time to hear my voice. I have had these words sealed on my heart for years. I have wanted to share the incredible wonders and good news that comes from knowing our heavenly Father. Our Father God has nothing but good for us. "For I know the plans I have for you," declares the Lord. "Plans to prosper you and not to harm you, plans to give you hope and a future" (Jeremiah 29:11 NIV). The purpose that He has given me is to make sure you know how wonderful He is and how, on the day I was born into eternity, I have been okay from that very moment. At that moment, it was set in place that the very thing that the enemy wanted to use for evil, He had already purposed for good. "But as for you, you meant evil against me; but God meant it for good, in order to bring it about as it is this day, to save many people alive" (Genesis 50:20 NKJV).*

*I saw you that night when you accepted Christ as your Savior. You admitted you were a sinner and accepted His salvation. You were happy that the Lord offered you a do-over. I watched you over the years as you struggled with the self-loathing and shame of what you did that day back in 1974. The enemy had you convinced that it was too great a sin. You thought that the only way to navigate through life with this was to make sure you kept it hidden. It was your secret sin. I just want you to never forget about the all-encompassing, wonderful grace that is offered to you in Jesus Christ. Mom, when you realized that we have a Savior that understands you intimately, you were able to finally came to yourself, and you saw the reality of what really happened. You remembered when the nurses said that those uncontrollable tears where just the result of the adjustment of your hormones. You knew, in your heart of hearts, that it had nothing to do with your hormones. You didn't know it at the time, but it was the Holy Spirit inside you that was grieving so deeply. You could not put it into words, and you could not explain it. How could anyone understand it? But God did. He knew what you were going through. He agonized for you. I saw Him cry for you, Mom. I saw Him when He saw your tears fall and your heart break. He cried with you because He understood the depth of your pain. He knew all about the pain of Satan's lie and deception. God also knew that it would be years before you would understand the truth of that moment. That truth is the moment I was aborted on earth I was received with rejoicing in heaven.*

*Now, Mom, I want you to know that I love you. The love I have for you is not out of ignorance. I am fully aware of what you did and why you did it. God shared with me just like He sees you and opened my heart and eyes into your heart from the inside. He doesn't see you like others see you. Because He is the Creator, there is a depth to His knowing. It is with that heavenly knowledge that He revealed to me the love that you had for me even when you didn't acknowledge it. There was a glimmering beam in the center of your heart, a beam that knew about God. He put that seed into your heart so that one day you would seek Him and understand the immense love that He has for you.*

*Mom, I want you to know that I know your heartbreak and the tough decision you had to make. I know it wasn't what you had planned, and it wasn't the way you had desired it; the circumstances around my conception were not what you had expected. When you were a little girl, thinking about being a mom and having children, this never entered your mind as the way it would happen. It should have been different, but it wasn't. It took all that you had within you to make the only decision that made sense to you at the time. But the Lord knows that there are many times in our lives that we think something is right when it really isn't, especially if you're not walking with Him. You didn't know His Word, His strength, His authority, His character—all that He has in store for us. His heart broke for you and all the other moms who didn't understand and made this choice. And so here comes the point that I want to share with you: what the purpose is for my life.*

*My life is to let you know that in light of all you have done and all you have thought and felt, God has sent me to tell you that I'm okay, that I love you, and that I love you with a heavenly love, a love that makes no sense, a love that only God can give me. Mom, He wants to you know that He loves you beyond words. He has prepared a way for your rescue. He has prepared a way of escape from the burdens and bondage by which the world's values that have so easily ensnare you. Mom, I come to you with a heart full of love and joy and anticipation. I have waited ever since the moment I was delivered into heaven for the hour that we would be reunited. I yearn to show you how much I love you. I want to reveal the beauty of heaven. Mom, it is amazing here. The colors are beyond anything you can imagine. Everyone loves one another. The atmosphere here doesn't feel like anything you have experienced. Oh, how I want you to see this! I know that when your time will be fulfilled and that time comes, the heavenly Father will have us come together. Only this time, you will be able to see me. You will see me! You will see me! I will be able to wrap my arms around you and hug you. You will know it's me. God has placed a special bond between us. That connection will allow us to know each other the minute we come in contact. God will orchestrate a perfect reunion moment. Because you see, that is what He wanted all along: for the three of us to be together—you, me, and Him.*

*O Lord, we crave Your presence, Your wonder. We long for You to be in our lives. We may not always understand what we see and experience, but God always brings meaning, understanding, beauty, healing, and forgiveness into our lives.*

*Mom, did you ever think that God was going to use this very act of rebellion to help you see Him and experience the depth of His forgiveness? Did you ever think that the death of your baby would be the life experience that would show you the overwhelming love of God that would bring eternal life of your soul? Did you ever think that the abandonment and betrayal that you felt at the moment of my death would bring you into the presence of the loving, all-embracing God of the universe? He embraces you with a heavenly embrace and loves you with an everlasting love that is pure and faithful and never ends.*

*I couldn't believe it. I am so thrilled that I am with Him. The fact that He was going to allow me to be part of His mighty plan to help you see the truth of Christ's salvation was breathtaking. That I would be used in this small way to help bring you to understand who God is and how He died for your sin is truly amazing! You spent years thinking that you had to pay for it. You lived a life full of the heartbreak, the regret, the embarrassment, the shame, the disgust, the disappointment, the confusion, the rationalization, all the time trying to justify it and make sense of it. All those struggles were an attempt to try to pay for it or reconcile for it. The longing to be whole, to have peace in your heart, was always present. Because before you made that decision, He had already created a way of escape, a way of forgiveness, a way of restitution, of redemption. Jesus paid it all! Oh, Mom, how wonderful it is that you no longer need to believe the lies of the enemy that want to keep you bound and trapped.*

*God doesn't waste anything, either. He uses everything for His glory and your benefit. I can't wait for our reunion. The lie that you killed me no longer applies because I'm alive and well in heaven. God has been with me the whole time and has been my heavenly Father. Oh, Mom, we are up here loving you.*

*Mom, do you know how many people on earth go through their lives and are never able to see and understand their mom's heart? Oh, what a blessing it's been for me to see the beauty you have in your heart, the love you have for others. O God, thank you for that, for revealing the truth to me of who she really is and who she is to others. Mom, I know you have had tears. I've asked Jesus about that. I would see you in your room with tears of sadness, regret, loneliness and discouragement. You see, we don't have those kinds of tears here. I don't know what that is like, but I can tell you that I can see that it looks like it hurts and is painful. The tears we have up here are with laughter and joy. Oh, how wonderful it is when those tears come. They are tears of joy and overwhelming gratitude in the salvation of Jesus Christ! Oh, Mom, I love you so much. I just want you to know that I'm fine, loved, and cared for. I have come to tell you we are all okay. There are many of us that God has received. They have all been delivered in heaven and eagerly await the moment their mothers finally grasp the wonderful truth: that they are all alive in heaven.*

## Julianne's Closing Prayer

*Precious Father, You are marvelous. You are supremely sovereign in all Your ways. I praise You for who You are and the outstanding plans that You have for our lives. You always intertwine them with Your perfect will. Your designs are always magnificent and without error. You are the Creator and God. Everyone in heaven sings You praises.*

*Heavenly Father, I thank You for Your love. Your love and holy kindness surround me. Your provision keeps me and amazes me. Your undying love for me is beyond comprehension. But You, O Lord, fathom all things. All of creation marvels at Your vast wisdom. Your insight of the entire universe is astounding. For You created altogether everything.*

*Jesus, I know that there are wounded souls seeking Your healing. I ask that You use the words to help guide them into Your complete forgiveness and healing, and that in the Holy Spirit's healing presence, they receive the salve for their sin-sick souls. Jesus, I ask that You touch all of the moms right now. Lord, open their eyes. Let them receive Your special healing today. Holy Spirit, I ask that You give them the encouragement and the strength to enable them to see the truth. Let them hear Your heart. Oh, Lord, how we want to be with our mothers again here in heaven, where You have loved us and nurtured us. Thank You for revealing our moms' hearts so we can see her the way You see them. You have given us a sweet and tender love for them. I pray that it surrounds her them now. Let them see the wonder and beauty of Your loving forgiveness. Let them embrace the truth: they are wonderfully made. Reassure them that we are well and tenderly taken care of. Let them see us basking in Your loving arms as we eagerly await our reunion with them in heaven.*

*Heavenly Father, I also know that there are others that have been affected by this life-changing decision. They too need to find truth as they seek understanding. Lord, I pray that You will give them the release and relief they so desperately pursue. Give them hearts of forgiveness and understanding. Regardless of the part they played, free them from the burden of shame, guilt, and regret that they may be carrying. Unshackle them from the bondage of the past and release them into abundant lives filled with freedom in their future. Please, Lord Jesus, give them peace everlasting.*

*Holy Spirit, thank You for giving me a chance to reveal myself to my mom, letting her know how much I love her, and showing me the truth of her situation. Thank You for showing me that there is nothing in it that You can't make right. There is nothing in it that You can't make beautiful again. I know that what Mom did was sin, and it was against your desired plan. But Lord God, You created a way for my mom to be forgiven for that sin. God, I want to thank You. You are giving me this amazing opportunity to tell her how much You love her. Thank You for revealing the truth so that she can leave this in her past and not drag it into her future. Thank You for making it her testimony and not her identity.*

*And, finally, thank You.*

*For you created my inmost being; you knit me together in my mother's womb. I praise you because I am fearfully and wonderfully made; your works are wonderful, I know that full well. My frame was not hidden from you when I was made in the secret place. When I was woven together in the depths of the earth, your eyes saw my unformed body. All the days ordained for me were written in your book before one of them came to be. How precious to me are your thoughts, O God! How vast is the sum of them. (Psalms 139:13–17 NIV)*

Photo of Flower

Photo of Bottom of Flower (base)

This is a picture of a flower given to me during the last Come to the Garden Retreat. The women had spent the previous year creating these beautiful flowers, each with a special message and Bible verse. At the end of the last evening session, we were all instructed to select our special flower, the flower specifically made for us and selected by the Holy Spirit. After a brief prayer of thanksgiving for such a marvelous weekend, I proceeded to randomly select my flower. Much to my amazement, the message and verse were:

Wonderfully Made (Psalm 139:14–16)

If you look closely, you will see a petal that has been crinkled. It forever reminds me that with all the cracks and wounds, with all the imperfections in my life, God still remarkably uses all of me. It is His brilliant way that He shows others how magnificent He is. My flaws are so important. Without them, God's eternal love and mercy could not be fully appreciated. He wastes nothing! All is wonderfully made for His glory.

Don't ever forget that our loving Father is always in every facet of our lives! He has prepared a plan and a place for us.

As you go forward in your life's journey, remember that your crinkles are God's way of reminding us of what He has done in our lives. Don't hide your imperfections—surrender them to God. He has a magnificent plan for them!

Enjoy the abundant life that you now have in Christ Jesus. Truly forgiven and set free!

Thank You, Lord, for all of me and
all of You.

# Acknowledgments

First and foremost, I must give acknowledgment to the true author of this book. This book was created out of obedience to the prompting of the Holy Spirit. His direction, strength, and inspiration were the guiding factors of this message. It is through His power, authority, and Word that this message was created. To God be the glory!

Along the way, God gave me some amazing people who demonstrated astounding support and encouragement. Had it not been for their unwavering love and friendship, this book might have taken a different direction. They all helped me stay focused and true to the Holy Spirit's prompting that I received in October 2017.

I have to begin at the beginning when it comes to acknowledgments: Christy Sawyer. What a wonderful woman of God. I have known Christy for many years and have watched as God has molded her and shaped her into a beautiful example of what a servant of God looks like. She is the leader of the River Dwellers ministry. There is no doubt in my mind that God used her that night at the Come to the River retreat in a remarkably special way by enabling her to speak so openly. She poured a powerful message of love and renewal into the lives of so many women. She spoke God's voice to me and changed the direction of my life. I want to thank you, Christy, for your faithful obedience to our Lord and Savior.

My greatest champion has been my husband, Billy Ray. From the beginning, Billy understood that this was something that the Lord was directing me to do. There was never a question in his mind that this book was to be written and published. His unwavering support and encouragement far exceeded anything I could have imagined. He has shown me amazing love and support like no other, from making sure I had a quiet place to be alone with God while writing to his never-ending words of encouragement. Sweetheart, you have by far been the wind beneath my wings. I love you!

To my children, Chris and Marcie. You have been a tremendous source of love and inspiration. You have continuously cheered me on to follow the Lord's leading during this journey. You have been openly supportive of this work, and for that I will forever be grateful. God has blessed you with hearts that are sensitive to the needs of others. Your lives have been an inspiration to me. My heart overflows with joy!

To my editors. I want to thank you for your contribution to this work. Most notably, I appreciated your expertise, discernment, and perspectives. Your love for the Lord gave a special devotion and commitment to the spirit of this work. You pored over this manuscript with great sensitivity and compassion. You used your professional skills to discover areas of improvement in grammar, punctuation, and sentence structure. But most of all, you were a constant source of professional encouragement, and for that I will always be in your debt.

There were many others who walked alongside me as I sought to be obedient to the Lord's leading. They have given me words of encouragement to my writing and spent hours listening to me talk through my journey. If I begin to list all of them, I'm sure I would miss someone, so please know that I value your friendship and thank

God for you daily. You all know who you are, and I thank you from the bottom of my heart.

Special note goes to my dear sister in Christ, Sannuella. She was with me the weekend this work was birthed. She knew firsthand what I experienced during that compelling retreat. She understood the powerful impact that this message would have on those wounded by their secret sin. It was with this insight that she courageously and lovingly read and critiqued my initial rough draft. I am so grateful that she was able to help me focus on the people who would read this and make sure that I was communicating the message with grace and truth. She is a dear sister in Christ, and I cherish what God has begun in our lives.

Last but certainly not least, I want to thank my Lord and Savior Jesus Christ! Only through His love, grace, and mercy could this testimony be given. His love for me is overwhelming, and I find it difficult to put into words the love I have for Him. Jesus's love is always far greater than any sin we may experience. Embrace Him and live!